Dessert First

Glimpses of Wisconsin Life

Gail Grenier

Dessert First is a work of nonfiction. Some names have been changed.

ISBN – 13: 978-1494875985
ISBN – 10: 1494875985

Produced in the United States of America.

Cover photo, of Michael Sweet and Gail Grenier Sweet in canoe, by Kathy Hynes Prochnow.

Cover design by Karen Cluppert of Not Just Words.

Proceeds from the sale of this book support HOPE Network for Single Mothers, a grassroots Milwaukee-area charity founded by the author in 1982.

Cataloging information provided by publisher:
Title: *Dessert First*
Subtitle: *Glimpses of Wisconsin Life*
Author: Grenier, Gail
          1950 –
Publisher: The Little Syndicate
          N80 W18397 Custer Lane
          Menomonee Falls, Wisconsin 53051
Date of publication: 2014
Subject: Wisconsin life 1950-2013

Also by Gail Grenier

Calling All Horses

Dog Woman

Don't Worry Baby

Blog
Gail Grenier Here

Website
GailGrenierSweet.com

A Note

Some essays and poems in this book are in print for the first time. Others were previously published in these newspapers:

The Ettrick Arrow
The Germantown Banner-Press
The Menomonee Falls News
The Milwaukee Journal Green Sheet
The Oxford Rural Rambler
The Platteville Journal
The Sussex-Lisbon-Lannon News

and these magazines:

Ambrosia
Creative Wisconsin Magazine
Inspiration Café
The Milwaukee Journal Wisconsin Magazine
Marriage and Family Living
Marriage Encounter
Mothering
Nurturing
Utne Reader

and these books:

Conscious Conception by Jeannine Parvati Baker
Wisconsin Poets' Calendar

and this blog:

Gail Grenier Here

Acknowledgments

Special thanks to my early readers: Elizabeth Boeck, Beth Hoffmann, Katie Kolberg Memmel, Anna Sweet, and Terre Woodward.

And thank you to my brother David Grenier and to my friend Karen Cluppert for scanning old family photographs.

*"'Tis a fearful thing to love
what death can touch."*

– Judah Halevi (circa 1075 – 1141)

Dedication

For Ted, Audrey and George Grenier,
who left this earth too early.
You taught me to live.

For my children and grandchildren,
who came to me through family and friendship.
If I were *really* good with words, I could tell you how
much you mean to me.

Dessert First

Glimpses of Wisconsin Life

Table of Desserts

With Charlie, Anna, Brian, Mike and morel mushrooms, May 2004

Introduction

As I write this, the outdoor temperature has reached – *almost* – zero degrees Fahrenheit. The thermometer read minus eight when I awoke this morning. I decided to skip snow-shoeing today, but I probably should have thrown on my several layers of clothing and headed out. It's breathtaking outside my window – sun bouncing off snow cover, deer tracks everywhere.

Wisconsin is a beautiful state, but it's no place for softies. Wisconsin people have grit. You grow up tough when you're raised with harsh north winds and stubborn immigrant tradition. I was nurtured by people who made me hearty and places that made me hardy. You'll meet some of my favorite folks – and places – in these pages.

Wisconsin grit held me up when my mother, father, and brother died in a car accident in 1978. Inspired by that event, I developed an outlook that is not uncommon in Wisconsin: Life is short and often hard, but it's full of desserts.

Everyone's desserts are different. I share mine in these pages: family and friends, nature and music, fun and folklore. Within the book's seven parts, there are seventy-seven short glimpses of Wisconsin life. Stories are in approximate chronological order within each section. You may read them any way you wish. Go from the end to the beginning, and you'll move from grieving to playing. Jump here or there, and you'll travel from woods to kitchens, from today back to the 1950s.

There are no demarcations in life. Time is a blur. Grief blends with play, play blends with sorrow, sorrow blends with joy. In grief itself, there is the joy that we loved and were loved.

Gail Grenier
Menomonee Falls, Wisconsin
December 29, 2013

Throughout the book you'll find bits of "lagniappe" – meaning "a little something extra" – an idea I learned years ago during a Cajun weekend at Folklore Village in Dodgeville, Wisconsin. My lagniappe for you is comprised of photos and words.

Part I
Playing

Flying a kite with brothers David and George, circa 1968
(Photo by Ted Grenier)

A Lesson from the Month of March, Long Ago

It was March at 7887 W. Beckett Avenue in Milwaukee, sometime during the 1950s. Danny and I walked over to the kitchen table, where Pop had placed two thin strips of balsa wood. One strip lay on top of the other so they formed the shape of a cross. Pop grabbed them and began fastening them to each other with string.

"This is the same string we're going to use to fly the kite," he explained, wrapping the string in an X-shape where the strips met. I watched, and Danny watched. Pop's hand moved fast like when he showed us yo-yo tricks. He could do walk-the-dog and double gerbil.

After Pop tied the string and cut it off, he put some dots of model airplane glue right in the center, under the string. Danny and I looked at each other and wrinkled our noses. We didn't like the smell.

"This has to dry for a while," Pop told us.

We followed him to the kitchen sink. I propped my elbows on the edge of the sink and leaned my chin into my cupped hands, watching him pour flour and water into a bowl. That was the bowl Mum used when she made cakes.

First Pop let me mix the flour and water. It was hard at first and then it got easier. Then my little brother Danny got a turn. I could tell it was really hard for him, but he was so small, what could you expect?

Pop added a bit more water, then did a couple of last sweeps with the big spoon, around and around. "There," he said. "We got most of the lumps out. Good library paste."

The library paste was really white and it looked like we could eat it. Sometimes when we played with Play-

Doh we really did take tiny bites, but we did it when Mum wasn't looking. Danny and I found out that Play-Doh tasted good only when it was fresh.

We didn't sneak any tastes of the library paste.

We went back to the table. Pop took a knife and put little notches in each balsa wood tip. Then he took more string and lashed it to each notch. When he was done, he had created a diamond shape in string that looked like the frame of a kite.

"Last comes the paper," he explained. He grabbed a sheet of yesterday's *Milwaukee Journal* Green Sheet and laid it on the table. I could see the funnies on the Green Sheet – my favorites, "Priscilla's Pop," and "Freddy," and all the others.

Pop set the kite frame onto the Green Sheet and carefully cut the paper to size, a little bigger than the frame. Next, he wrapped the newspaper around the edges of the string. I watched his thick fingers slowly crease the paper and press it down. I saw how his gold ring shone. I looked at the freckles and the tiny red hairs on his hands.

From time to time he took a break for a puff of his cigarette that was sitting in an ashtray, smoke snaking upward.

"Now comes the fun part," Pop said.

He put his big finger right into the library paste and showed us how to smear the paste onto the newspaper so it would stick to itself around the string-frame.

First Danny smeared the paste, then I did, then Danny did, then I did. Pop made sure all the paper edges were stuck tight to each other. Now it really looked like a kite, the shape of a big diamond. I liked the color of the Green Sheet. The funnies looked strange going sideways and getting cut off at slanted points.

We didn't decorate the kite with crayons, but that would have been fun.

Pop attached two special strings to the kite. "This is the yoke," he said. To the yoke he attached the kite string that was wound at one end around a stubby stick. Last, he tied a couple of his old ties onto the bottom point of the kite frame. "This is the tail. If it's windy tomorrow, we might need more ties."

The painful part was letting the paste dry. Pop didn't want to fly the kite until the next morning, to be safe. It was Saturday night. Danny and I had to take a bath and put on our jammies. All clean, we jumped up and down on our parents' big bed for a while, then watched a little of "Lawrence Welk" with Mum and Pop, then went to bed with antsy hearts. Morning would never come.

But it did. Before breakfast and before church we ran across the street with Pop, to the vacant lot. He said, "This is a perfect wind. Watch."

Danny and I watched as he held the kite over his head and ran. Pop could run fast. Suddenly he let go of the kite and it climbed, up and up into the air. High.

That was good, but not as good as when Pop let me hold the string. I could feel the kite tug and tug. It was strong, like a living person. I watched it sail in the blue sky. Sometimes it swooped down and I'd get scared. Pop said, "Pull back." I did, and the kite corrected itself. It went even higher.

Danny got a turn too, but Pop had to help him.

Eventually there were more kids in the family – Sally and David. I don't remember if Pop made kites with them, but he surely took them kite-flying.

When I was a teenager, my mother had another baby. His name was George and I got to show him how to fly a kite. It felt good to be the teacher. I loved seeing George's eyes become bright as the kite soared. When it dipped, I told him, "Pull back." He did.

I grew up, married, and had three kids. I had a lot of fun with them, but we never made a kite together. Every March when the wind blows, I wonder why.

Maybe I was "too busy." Maybe I didn't have confidence in my kite-making skills. Pop had died young and I had no idea where to go for directions.

Now I have four of my own grandchildren and eight more whom I "adopted." I'm still busy, but I'm not too busy to see each one of them every week or two. We do a lot of the things I used to do with my own kids – toss a ball in spring, break paths through woods in summer, tramp through corn fields in fall, go sledding in winter. Indoors, we read and draw and spin hula-hoops. For special occasions, I take them to the movies and we eat big tubs of popcorn. For sleepovers, we watch my collection of Betty Boop, Felix the Cat, and Popeye cartoons.

I'm making a promise to myself. I'm going to buy some balsa wood. I'm getting out the flour, the water, the newspaper. Because I realize now that making a kite is making memories.

We may even decorate it with crayons.

[2013]

In the mid-seventies, Mike and I lived with our two sons in a tiny house surrounded by farm fields in the Town of Lisbon. When Pop visited, we'd sit on our front porch and play a game he remembered from his childhood: taking turns predicting whether the next car to pass would be a Ford or a Chevy.

Pretending

When I was nine years old, I told my across-Beckett-Avenue neighbor Peggy Potter that I could fly.

"For real?" she asked.

"For real," I said.

Peggy was only eight. Karen Schemer, who lived on Appleton Avenue a block away, was also eight.

"I can fly," I told Karen.

"You can?"

"Yup."

My brother Danny was seven. I'm not sure if he bought it entirely, but I told him the same story. He told his bicycle gang – Mike Delaney, Denny Stauber, and his brother Dale.

Now there were six kids younger than I was who believed I could fly. My challenge was to convince an older kid: Randy, who was Peggy's big brother. He was eleven. I had a little problem with Randy. The previous fall he told me there was no Santa Claus. I told him there was so a Santa Claus, and then I beat my fists on his chest until he ran away.

"You can't fly," he said.

"Can too."

"Let's see."

"Okay."

Randy and I set the place and day and time: my house, tomorrow, 4:00 pm. I alerted the other neighborhood kids.

The next day right before 4:00, I waited, sitting on the green-and-white metal glider on our side porch. Back and forth, back and forth I glided with a *squeak* on each glide. I listened to my mother inside, clattering pots and pans while she made supper. I heard my little sister and baby brother pestering her.

The kids arrived at our house by foot or bike from the corners of the neighborhood: Peggy; Karen; my brother Danny and his gang Mike, Denny, and Dale; and last of all, Randy the big kid. They followed me down the steps to our basement rec room.

Nobody said anything.

I grabbed an old wooden chair full of paint splotches and set it in the center of the room, away from the upright piano and the bar and the couch with the scratchy upholstery.

The kids formed a lopsided circle around me.

"Let's see," Randy said.

"Okay."

The kids pressed forward a bit, still silent. It would be a hard flight for me, clearing their heads while gliding under the dropped rec room ceiling.

I put my two feet firmly on the seat of that old chair. I straightened myself to my full height, still well below the ceiling. I let go of the back of the chair. I extended my arms, squatted down to create momentum, and leaped straight out –

– and straight down to the floor, *plop*, squarely on my feet.

I looked around at the circle of eyes on me, especially on the eyes of Randy the big kid.

"It didn't work today," I explained.

Nobody, not even Randy, said anything as we clattered up the steps and back outside into the late afternoon sunshine. I think they had been pretending as hard as I had.

[2006]

There are few things as real as a child's imagination.

Mice Wearing Clothes

1936
little prairie town
Ellie and Ruth Miller
two sisters, playing,
search under garage floorboards, find baby mice.

Ellie shrinks backward,
Ruth smiles,
cradles mice babies,
names them,
makes a little mouse house,
sews tiny coats and hats, dresses the mice.

Days later
neighbor Mrs. MacGoogan
of white gloves and hats
and bad-tasting pies,
the very proper Mrs. MacGoogan
bringing over warm rhubarb pie
shrieks, "Mrs. Miller! Mrs. Miller!"

Ellie and Ruth's ma
wide-eyed,
runs outside,
finds the very proper Mrs. MacGoogan
red-faced,
out of breath in the front yard,
steaming pie smashed at her feet,
Ruth sitting nearby under a tree.

Mrs. MacGoogan shrieks,
"Mrs. Miller, I think I've lost my mind –
I just saw a mouse wearing clothes!"

1996
Menomonee Falls
Arleen and I
two friends
go biking to the quarry lake where
Arleen tells me about
mice wearing clothes,
as old Ellie told her
last night.
Arleen tells me about
the very proper Mrs. MacGoogan
while we climb our big quarry rock.
We buckle, laughing,
I lose balance,
almost fall, laughing,
into corduroy ripples
blowing on the surface of cold quarry water below.

I wipe tears and Arleen grabs me
hugs me
"I feel like I just laughed with my sister,"
she says, "How we used to laugh."

I remember
two summers gone
Arleen and I drove to the nursing home
in Minnesota
where Arleen's sister lives,
Arleen's sister Carrie,
curled up now,
twelve years sleeping – coma sleeping.
I remember
watching Arleen stroke Carrie's hair,
        talk to her,
        no laughter.

I have Arleen
and she has me –

we bike together
to the quarry lake.
We sit on our rock,
gaze at the sky in water,
gaze at ripples on water,
gaze at trout below,
listen to fishermen laugh
as they tell stories
funny stories
like the tale of
mice wearing clothes –
they tell their stories
and find their families where they make them.

As we do.

[1996]

Of our friendship, my friend Terre Woodward says, "It seems we grew on the same tree.

Collision!

Today I bonded more than ever before with my biking buddy Arleen Hollenhorst. Today we fell together on the Bugline trail in Menomonee Falls.

I wonder if our accident had anything to do with the fact that we talked about accidents for half of our nine-mile ride. Could we have jinxed ourselves?

First I told Arleen about how my daughter Anna broke her arm Sunday on a trampoline.

Then she told me the story of how she was the first at an accident scene this month. Arleen sat with the gravely injured woman until help arrived.

Then I told her about coming upon a severed leg first and an accident scene second, six hours away from home driving back to Wisconsin from Florida. If only we had gone to see Lincoln's birthplace like I wanted to, we would have never come upon the leg, but *no*, everyone had stable call, so we skipped the tourist attraction and encountered the horror. It was a *long* six hours to our front door.

But Arleen and I weren't talking about accidents when our own collision occurred. No, we were talking about sex. We were pretty deep into the topic when our handlebars linked and *time ... slowed ... down.*

I thought surely I could get my handlebar out of hers. I had to face the fact that I was mistaken in that assumption when I realized we were both going down, down, down, and worst of all, I was falling *onto* my friend.

It all probably took one second, but it felt like slow motion: the locking of the handlebars, the slow fall, the gradual slide along the gravel, the feeling of her body beneath mine, and finally the shock at seeing our bikes tangled together on the ground.

After that, time sped up to normal pace. And we *laughed.* We had determined that nothing was broken on us, and untangled our bicycles, when a couple biked up to us and asked if we were all right. Arleen was bleeding from several places but we laughed and said we were okay. We were both relieved they didn't see us fall – embarrassment hurts worst of all.

We had to walk the half-mile home because Arleen's cruiser was horribly beat up. We got to my house and cleaned our wounds. Arleen's legs looked as if they had been attacked by a dinner fork. It was time for bandages and gauze.

My neighbor straightened Arleen's handlebars. Then my ever-game biking buddy, age 50, hopped back onto her one-speed.

Before she left for her home, Arleen let out one last laugh and said, "Two old ladies on bikes, talking about sex – after all these years we biked and never fell!"

There's a lesson in there somewhere.

[1997]

Friendship is a gift we give ourselves.

Twelve-Almost-Thirteen

Anna had her first boy-girl party last Friday. I dropped my normal objections to coed parties for seventh graders because we have a new above-ground swimming pool. I decided that a swimming party (with "Bring water pistols" on the invitation) would allow kids to be kids, much more than those gooney dances they have in middle school.

The party turned out to be four hours of high entertainment for my husband and me. For most of those hours, it was all-out water war between the boys and the girls. Anna invited every kid in her class at St. Mary's in Menomonee Falls. All but a few showed up. So we had eighteen boys and eighteen girls, all aged twelve-almost-thirteen, engaged in battle.

Three boys came ultra-prepared. When I asked them what the backpacks and big cooler were for, they confessed that they spent an hour before the party filling water balloons at home. Their ammo was stuffed into the backpacks and the cooler.

Very quickly in the water war, our hayloft became contested territory. First the girl army occupied it, then the boy army. Sometimes they'd forget about lobbing water grenades at each other and take turns jumping out of the hayloft: a big thrill for kids without barns. I kept praying for no broken legs – I've had enough of casts this summer.

I wonder if things will be different if Anna throws a swimming party at the end of the school year. At age twelve, kids still: grabbed four cookies at once; flung their own bodies over the side of the pool and into the water; managed to get covered in mud; never once engaged in boy-girl conversation except to argue over who got the most pizza; chased and held our chickens; and trooped across our road to see the dead skunk.

My own sons are nineteen and twenty-one, and I had forgotten what it's like to have a twelve-year-old boy around. Boys that age have boats, not feet; and they clump, they don't walk, through the house. The fellas left behind a couple of pairs of jockey shorts and tube socks that I know will never be claimed.

And these, girls, are your dreamboats of the future.

[1997]

I had Anna when Charlie was eight-and-a-half and Brian was six-and-a-half. Anna was my "Change of mind" baby.

'Tis Right and Verily So, My Lord

I'll never know if my day in virgin sacrifice garb was as daunting as my husband's day in tights.

It started when my son Charlie's Romanian folk dance troupe was invited to perform for the coronet feast of the Southeast Wisconsin Society for Creative Anachronism (SCA). Charlie asked if we'd like to see the show, but added that we'd have to wear medieval garb.

I managed to borrow costumes from Falls Patio Players, our local theatre group. I had purchased costume patterns, but was relieved I wouldn't have to wrestle my sewing machine. The outfits were three lovely dresses and floral wreath headpieces, described by costume designer Roger Bochek as "virgin sacrifice costumes."

My daughter Anna and her best friend Colleen are lithe young teens with room to spare in the bodice department. I took a needle and thread and sewed them into their dresses. The same empire-waist gown on me created an effect I can only describe as a flesh pillow. I remedied that with a bit of old lace curtain strategically placed between bosom and costume.

My husband Mike's head attire must have been approved by the Ministry of Funny Hats. His long tunic had puffy sleeves trimmed in gold. Beneath the tunic he wore white tights.

The tunic was basically a dress; Mike didn't know how to approach it. He ripped out the zipper putting it on – safety pins to the rescue. He grumbled as he went to the bathroom before we left: "Probably the last time I'll get to go all day."

I started laughing. "It's just like a dress and pantyhose! You pull up the dress and pull down the hose, and you can go any time."

Our son Brian's reluctance to don a costume caused him to miss a two-hour meaty feast and a lively coronet tournament, where entrants battled to earn titles for themselves and their consorts. The fighters used various modified medieval weapons plus chain mail, shields, padding, and helmets.

It took effort to navigate with sleeves that extended to my knees and with a dress train that I had to maneuver through other dress trains.

I was surprised to learn that SCA is an international phenomenon. Besides speaking using a lot of "my lords," "my ladies" and "good gentles," SCA members strive to rekindle the lost ideals of chivalry, courtesy and honor. The nation's principalities are preparing for "war." Loser gets Philadelphia. (I'm not sure what the winner gets.)

Mike enjoyed the ambiance, but not the garb. He was conscious all day of keeping the front of his tunic closed. When he got home, he ripped off those white tights and scratched his itchy legs. He didn't get much sympathy from me.

"Now thou knowest verily what it is like to be a woman," said I.

[2000]

If you get married in Wisconsin and they don't play a polka at the reception, your marriage is automatically annulled.

Root Beer Popsicle, 95 Degrees

If motherhood means
revisiting childhood,
then grandmotherhood means
revisiting motherhood and
revisiting
childhood.

Today it was 95 degrees out
when my grandson Oliver and I walked
together
barefoot on
the very warm Milwaukee sidewalk,
like the very warm Milwaukee sidewalks of my
    childhood,
        concrete bits sparkling like stars in sunlight.

And suddenly I
craved a root beer popsicle
like the ones we used to eat –
haven't had a
root beer popsicle in
maybe
45 years.

Thanks, Oliver.

[2006]

*Sidewalks in Milwaukee are as beautiful in their own
way as farmers' fields in Markesan.*

Entering the Magical World of a Child

Once a week, I have a day with my grandkids. This is a tradition of eight years, one I cherish. Every grandkid day is different. They're all funny, but they're not all magical. Magical is when a child forgets you're there – or doesn't care – and you get a chance to peek into the amazing world of the child's imagination, which is *very real* to the child.

If you think back, very hard, to your own childhood, you will remember the feeling that the imaginary is real, perhaps more real than everyday life.

This week's grandkid visit was a magical one. Oliver (age seven) and Liam (age two) were playing in the family room, which is just two steps up from the basement. I went into the basement for a moment, and when I came back, Oliver and Liam were huddled together beside the open doorway between the family room and the basement.

At first I thought they were hiding there to startle me with "Boo!" – but not so. They ignored me. They kept looking past me, into the basement, as if someone were lurking there. Each boy held a thingie made of Tinker Toys.

"What's going on?" I asked.

"We're shooting some bad guys," Oliver explained quietly.

"Oh." I stood there. Quiet. Then I backed away to the opposite side of the open doorway.

Oliver stood frozen, cautious, out of sight of the bad guys. Occasionally he snatched a glance into the basement, then tucked his head back. He was taking no chances.

Suddenly he reached forward with his Tinker Toy thingie and aimed it into the basement. I figured out that the Tinker Toy thingie was a gun when he nailed a bunch of bad guys with it. It made machine gun sounds that emanated from Oliver's mouth. Liam did whatever Oliver did, although his sound effects weren't as perfected.

Oliver looked up at me with big serious eyes and said, "We'll protect you."

"Good," I said.

He shot some more.

"Are they all gone?" I asked.

"There's one left." He shot again. That was it. With the enemy vanquished, the boys put their guns into the block box. We settled onto the couch to read books. For a minute, I was in their world. I don't know how I gained entry this time, but I have a hunch that a light tread is required.

[2013]

Reading to Liam and Oliver, 2012 (Photo by Rachl Sweet)

When we grandmothers play with our grandchildren, it's a ruse. All we really want to do is hug them and squeeze them and kiss them.

Secret of Happiness

This past Thursday, I learned again what I believe is true: kids don't need *things* to be happy. That is, they don't need gadgets or fancy toys or lessons or groups or guided this or that.

This is what happened: Our two grandsons busied themselves while my husband, Mike, and I chatted in one of the Milwaukee Domes (a huge indoor horticultural park) with our son Brian and his wife Rae. The dome was filled with people enjoying a band.

Without words, Oliver (age eight) started making a pattern on the cobblestones, using wood chips from the path. Immediately, Liam (age two) started fetching chips and delivering them to Oliver, back and forth. Oliver continued making the pattern.

"What are you making?" I asked Oliver.

"It's a fence to show Liam's and my territory," he explained.

After a few minutes, a little girl joined in. Quietly, she formed what became the start of an assembly line. She picked up two wood chips, then handed them to Liam. Liam walked the chips over to Oliver and put them down on the ground near where Oliver was working. Oliver picked up the chips and added them to his construction project.

This went on for about fifteen or twenty minutes, all without words. Finally I asked the little girl her name and age. She was Wendy, she said, and she was six, and her mom and nana were over there.

The children worked silently for a while more. Finally Wendy asked Oliver, "What are we making?" I don't remember what he answered. Soon after that, Wendy ran off.

The creation was a beautiful chain of wood chips with some height – like a stone wall along a farmer's winding field row in Ireland. Oliver announced that it was now a train track. He gave Liam one chip, and he took a chip, and they drove their chip-trains along the track.

Soon it was time to go. We all picked up the chips and threw them back on the path.

The happiness and concentration of the children reminded me of the movie "Babies," where the little African child is so content to play with bones and dirt.

It also brought to mind a quotation about dealing with children that I have loved since hearing it back when I was learning to be a teacher at Marquette University: "Do not save time; waste it" (Jean-Jacques Rousseau).

Dismantling the train track and throwing the wood chips back on the path made me think of the Buddhist monks who make annual visits to Waukesha County Technical College, where I teach. They work for about a week to create a sacred mandala "painting" out of colored sand. My back feels tired as I watch them stoop over their work. They carefully coax sand from little pourers onto a table where the mandala takes shape. When they are finished making the mandala, they dump the sand into a river – to demonstrate the impermanence of everything we do, and the importance of non-attachment.

Liam and Oliver were perfectly happy to destroy what had taken about a half-hour to create. Their joy was in the *doing*. And as Wendy demonstrated by her question to Oliver, it didn't matter what they were making, only that they were making it.

It's an old bit of wisdom, and I believe it's true, that the best way to be with children is to focus on *process*, not product.

True happiness doesn't come from *things*. This is true for adults as well as children, I think.

[2013]

Part Two
Loving

With adopted mom Nancy Reinsvold – and tomato, 2012

Holy Hill Honeymoon

It was Monday, August 14, 1972, and Mike and I had gotten married on Saturday. We were headed to Holy Hill, a shrine in Hubertus, Wisconsin, for our honeymoon.

The real reason for our trip to Holy Hill was to test the van we had customized for our post-wedding odyssey. We'd planned that the first thing we were going to do after we got married was to get the heck out of this cold state of Wisconsin. We were going to drive south and stop and look for jobs when it got warm enough for us. Ironic considering that it was 85 degrees in Milwaukee at the time.

We had our college degrees, a thousand bucks in wedding gift money, and a dream.

Earlier that summer, we had found a used 1962 Chevy Corvair van in the want ads, and bought it for $800. It was a utility van from the era before luxury vans. It was painted a sort of dark shade of green not quite as appealing as army green. It had no cup holders and no windows on the sides. It had a rear engine and a stick shift, and *usually* three gears on the floor.

We didn't find out about that elusive second gear until almost a month later, somewhere in the Ozarks, where the engine's place in the rear prevented the van from blowing up ... but that's another story.

Mike's parents, Jerry and Lenora, were handy. They helped us customize the van. We made it our first home – a little traveling home. Jerry devised a plywood platform for our mattress. "More bounce per ounce," he said to Mike during the construction – probably the raciest thing Jerry ever said to his son. You could flip the plywood upward and fasten it by a hook to the ceiling. Then a little table would pop out for eating. We had a couple of card table chairs to use at the table. Jerry snapped nylon screening to the side door opening, and Lenora sewed a zipper into the screen so we could sleep in breezy comfort on a summer evening.

I decorated the ceiling of the van with psychedelic fabric I had found – blue, yellow, red, and purple stars and rainbows. I made a pillow to match.

We loaded our clothes into a little dresser left over from Mike's babyhood. In the way-back of the van were small shelves where we kept a camp cook set we had found at Sherper's Army surplus store in Hales Corners, along with our library, which consisted of the Holy Bible and the complete works of J.D. Salinger. We had a gas camp cooker and a toilet seat on folding legs that we stashed in back somewhere.

We were set.

We spent so much time getting our van ready that we completely forgot about planning a honeymoon, much less lodging for the first night of our marriage. I told Mike to book the closest hotel to our wedding reception because I knew we wouldn't feel like driving far. He booked a night at the Suburban Hotel. Our friend Gail Hills was horrified. "That's where people go for an hour," she said. "That's a real 'Squeaky Springs Hotel.'"

Well, the Suburban was fine for us – we weren't noticing our surroundings that night. As I recall, we did everything except couple from the chandelier. Finally! Sex was legal!

We opened our gifts on Sunday. In private that morning, my grandmother "Mémère" said, "What *happened* to you, Gail?" as she gazed forlornly at my bosom. I explained to her, "I wore a padded bra under my wedding dress, Mémère."

Monday it was time to test drive the van. Mike suggested taking a little camping honeymoon at Holy Hill, where he had camped as a Boy Scout. Sounded fine to me. Someone gave us a gallon of wine, and we were ready to go.

We made it to Holy Hill with no trouble. Mike rang the rectory bell and asked one of the friars if we could camp for a few days at the base of the hill, right near the start of the Stations.

"Well, I don't know," the friar said. "I'll have to go ask the cook."

The cook said yes, and our Holy Hill honeymoon began.

The weather was balmy, we were alone, the air was fresh, and the trees were bursting with August. We wandered through the woods, happy with our peace and quiet. We shared a hearty meal of ground beef, cream of mushroom soup, and canned corn, a "Michael meal" from Mike's college apartment days. We drank some wine.

I don't remember using the plastic toilet seat on folding legs, but I must have, since there are no restrooms at the base of Holy Hill. Everything was perfect except for the flies, but we had hung a strip of sticky flypaper just inside our love nest. We left the two side doors wide open and zipped shut our nylon screening, ready to enjoy a soft summer night.

But I couldn't fall asleep. I lay in the dark – and I do mean pitch black dark – there were no lights anywhere. All I could think about was the fact that we were surrounded by those big woods and all those big kettles and moraines and surely there must be big bears wandering. Big bears could surely tear through our piddly little net and grab us and devour us, slowly, oh the thought of being eaten bit by bit. It would be better to be shot, you could get it over with right away. Being eaten would be such a *long* torture.

I got scareder and scareder of bears as Mike lay next to me snoring. Finally I woke him up. "Mike," I said, "I'm scared of *bears*."

I don't remember what he said, but somehow he assured me that there were no bears in these woods. Finally I joined him, spoon-style, in a deep, dark sleep.

The next thing I knew, there was a horrible pounding, pounding, pounding, and a bright light streaming through the black night right onto me and Mike. Mike always sleeps harder than I do, which means he wakes with more of a shock. He bolted right up out of our little bed and hit his head on the ceiling and got his hair all entangled with the flypaper.

"What? What?" he mumbled, naked and disoriented.

"Police!" said the voice behind the big beam of light.

Oh, man, this was like a bad flashback to the time of "watching submarine races" at the lakefront. We had to explain to the cop that we were newlyweds on our honeymoon and the friars had given us permission to camp there. The cop explained that neighbors had complained that night about bikers making a lot of noise in the area. Well, we hadn't heard anything – not bikers, not bears. Nothing.

The cop finally left. Mike was humiliated about the whole naked flypaper thing, but eventually we fell again into a deep dark sleep.

When we woke, there was music and talking. Music and talking? What happened to the solitude of the night before? It was a Tuesday morning – what could it be?

Mike and I gradually shook the sleep out of our heads and realized we were surrounded. We also realized our van was wide open and only a little screen separated us from whoever was out there. We slunk horizontally into our clothes, zipped open the screen, and walked out ...

... into the middle of a Greek picnic. There were children playing, ladies preparing food, and lots of Greek men with fierce mustaches. No one spoke English, but somehow we figured out that this family came to the same site on the same day every year. They weren't going to let a little thing like a parked, occupied van get in the way of their tradition.

We moved the van.

And started our marriage.

[2005]

With Mike, brothers David and George, neighbor kids, and our 1962 Chevy Corvan – August 13, 1972

I tell newlyweds that the secret to staying married is to not get divorced every time you break up.

Lucky Teach

Wednesday, Sept. 16, 1992, at Erin's house.

It's my first day homebound-teaching Erin, who is seven years old and recovering from a bone marrow transplant which we hope will lick her tenacious leukemia once and for all.

I almost didn't recognize Erin when I first saw her. She used to be a classic blonde, with blond brows and blond lashes, like her brother and sister. But medical treatments have caused her hair to fall out, and it's growing back dark. Now her eyes have a dreamy Liz Taylor look – blue with dark fringes. Until her hair is grown in completely, she wears a short wig dressed up with bows.

I've known Erin since she was about three years old. The first time I saw her was in our church nursery: a tiny towhead climbing up a ladder and sliding down a slide again and again, maneuvering with arms too short for her little body and hands bent slightly inward. Nothing was going to stop Erin, not even a so-called disability. *She's a scrapper*, I thought. I didn't realize it then, but the image of the ladder and slide was an appropriate symbol for Erin, who would experience a lifetime's worth of medical ups and downs before she reached the age of eight.

Erin and my daughter Anna enrolled in St. Mary's school in Menomonee Falls. When they were in the first grade, I became their Brownie leader. I found Erin to be a pleasure to have in our troop of twenty-four girls. She always had a smile on her face.

Last December, Erin played the role of the Virgin Mary in St. Mary's school Christmas musical. She was a tiny Mary in blue and white, recreating my childhood image of the nativity scene. She and her miniature Joseph sang "Still, still, still" so true that I used up all my film shooting pictures of them – as if a snapshot could capture their sweet voices.

Last March, Erin experienced a recurrence of the leukemia that had stricken her when she was younger. It was a rough time for everyone who loved her. I took it harder than I had taken deaths in my family. I was angry with God. I asked God "Why?" Perhaps Erin's illness was too threatening for me because she was the same age as my own little girl.

In July, Erin underwent the marrow transplant. She was sent home after spending more than a month at Children's Hospital in Milwaukee. Now she must return each week for medication and check-ups. She is very susceptible to infection at this point; she can't be exposed to people until she is much stronger. She may be away from the school building for a year. I wash my hands before our lessons.

I had many emotions when I was hired to be Erin's teacher – most of all I felt honored – but I also experienced some trepidation. I was afraid to grow close to her and then "lose" her. However, seeing her in her own home, gobbling up schoolwork, helps me think positive. And I remind myself that all of us living are actually dying a little every day. It's a process.

Erin seems very serious; maybe that's because she's been around only adults for the past couple of months. I asked her if she wanted to call me "Gail" or my married name, and she chose "Gail." I felt like hugging her goodbye today after our lessons, but I held back because I was afraid to take chances with germs.

Friday, September 18, 1992
For "recess" or "phy ed" or "break," Erin and I run up and down the driveway. We started with two round trips and we've progressed to three. We're both breathless when we finish. We laugh about the neighbors who must think we're crazy. We took a "field

trip" to the public library, which was nearly empty in the middle of the day. Still, Erin had to cover her face with a surgical mask, something she hates to do. People stare, she said, and it's embarrassing. She's planning to trick-or-treat as a surgeon so she can wear the mask and not feel odd. I was relieved when Mary Lou, her mother, said I could hug Erin.

"Most danger is from the mouth and hands," Mary Lou explained. Erin and I hugged goodbye today. It felt right.

Tuesday September 22, 1992

Erin is a Catholic school student so it's okay for us to pray together; that feels right, too. Erin likes to talk about the miracle of Jesus raising the young girl from the dead. Today when we prepared to pray, I suggested visualizing her body cells becoming stronger. But Erin piped in about Brian, a boy she met at the hospital. She wants to pray for *him*, not for herself. So we did.

Hospital chat naturally filters into our lessons. "Sometimes good things happen in the hospital and sometimes bad things happen," Erin said. For language class, Erin had to write about her favorite thing from summer. She said she was in the hospital most of the summer. "My mom and Brian's mom called it 'the summer from hell'," Erin told me. Instead, she wrote about last May, when she and her mother received a gift trip to Disney World through American Dream Flight. Erin loved it even though it was "very very very hot."

We rode bikes until she tired. Afterward, she said, "That was some recess!" We both agreed home school is better than regular school because both of us, teacher and student, can chew gum – and we love our gum. Plus, Erin likes the fact that she never has to *wait* for anything.

Erin has a cold. I'm worried about her; "little" illnesses can be big trouble for her.

Wednesday, September 23, 1992

Erin's classmates send cards and letters and things made with glue and glitter and little packages full of treasures dredged from bedroom shelves. She reads every message before lessons begin. And she writes back.

Erin is feverish and her breathing is labored. Yesterday she wore two sweatshirts but still shivered almost the whole three hours we worked together. We sat on the floor like two cats in the hot sunny window, and Mary Lou turned on the heat. But even fever couldn't keep Erin from her lessons. She's a scrapper.

This was the end of our second week together. She started lessons two and a half weeks behind her peers, but after twelve hours one-on-one, she's almost caught up. I gave her an end-of-the-week reward: a pack of bubble gum, her favorite treat, and a mini-storybook.

We hugged goodbye from a distance because I was afraid to make her more ill with any germs that might be on me. We stretched our arms to each other and scrunched our faces and grunted as if we were giving each other big bear hugs.

Sunday, September 27, 1992

Today Erin checked into Children's Hospital. Besides having a bad cold, she has developed an infection in the catheter that is in her chest. The catheter is for drawing blood and for intravenous medicine. The kids at the hospital call these catheters their "charleys," and they consider them a nuisance but "better than getting poked all the time."

Monday, September 28, 1992

My friend Donna, a teacher of emotionally disturbed children, described the misery she's been going through with some students. She shared with me how she calmed herself in prayer and received

34

what she considered words from God: "They're MY kids. Just take care of 'em." *Our children don't "belong" to us*: what a philosophy for me as Erin's teacher, and what a philosophy for her parents too, who have lived for years on a medical roller coaster.

Thursday, October 1, 1992

Play is children's work. Today and Monday Erin and I played school in her hospital room. She's doing much better, but her teacher wasn't doing too well Monday. It was my first visit to Children's Hospital: my first encounter with little bald kids walking around the halls with IVs and portable medicine-drip stands. It was hard to see. But today I felt more relaxed, like Erin's dad, who calls the hospital "a hotel with medicine," according to Erin.

Erin flips twelve-letter medical terms around like a pro. She discusses her medications and procedures with the nurses, and they talk to her as if they're accustomed to her understanding everything. She told me she'd like to be a nurse when she grows up. For school, Erin had to survey people about their favorite endangered species. She polled every nurse and technician who came into her room. The only time Erin was too shy to ask was when a new attendant entered. She knows many staffers by name, and she has her favorites.

Erin attacked schoolwork with her customary diligence. To help her lighten up a bit, I gave her two joke books and assigned her homework: "Tell jokes."

We spent a long time doing addition and subtraction drills. I thought, *What if she's dying? What difference does math make?* But I realize this isn't about math; teaching is my way of being with Erin. Our phy ed took the form of walks down the hallways, with Erin tugging her medicine-drip pole along with her. She showed me the wondrous play room that was full of big, colorful climbing toys and art supplies.

When we prayed today, we prayed for others again. "I'm sick of praying for myself," Erin said.

Thursday, October 8, 1992

Since coming home from the hospital, Erin is a new person. I didn't realize her previous seriousness was related in part to simply not feeling good. Now Erin needs no help to lighten up. She gets the contagious giggles. Her little sister Annie jumped on the couch as their mother was cleaning it, and Erin burst out laughing. I caught the joke too, and soon Mary Lou was giggling with all of us. Mary Lou's eyes met mine and I knew we were laughing for another reason: it was wonderful to hear Erin laugh.

Erin said, "I put a charley on my toy Dalmatian dog." More giggles.

She said the good thing about developing the infection in her charley was that she got it out a month early.

For math, we played Blackjack (more fun than addition drills). Erin caught on to the game right away and had a long streak of beginner's luck. I called her a "whippersnapper" for beating an old lady. She picked up on that and began calling me "Old Lady." When I started winning, she said, "I'm gonna get you, Old Lady." Sometimes she calls me "Teach."

Erin went outside and gave me a show: a variety of hilariously contorted funny faces through the window. When we needed a break, Erin played the CD of "Beauty and the Beast." She knows every word. Soon Annie, Erin, and I were dancing around the family room in a gloriously silly ballet, Erin belting out the songs at the top of her lungs, using one of Annie's teeny tennis shoes as her microphone. I grabbed the other sneaker, which Annie had discarded, and performed as a do-wop background singer.

Then Erin switched to a Whitney Houston CD. Our performance became aerobic. When I got wild, Erin cheered me on: "*Go*, Gail!" Erin squinched her eyes and sang with fervor: "I wanna dance with somebody who loves me!" At the crescendo, she jumped onto the couch and let it rip. I cheered, "*Go*, Erin!" When we finished dancing, we were both breathless. She told me she wants to be a singer and dancer when she grows up, and informed me that singers really close their eyes like she did, "to show feeling."

We went outside for science and wandered along the tree line, admiring wild flowers and things like moss on rocks. Erin noted everything in her "Woods Diary." What a natural, quiet way to learn! I recalled a saying of the French philosopher Jean-Jacques Rousseau: "Do not save time; waste it."

Lying on the sun-warmed deck, Erin told me her recurrent dream: "I'm riding a dolphin at Disney World and I have my hair and I don't have a charley and I feel good," she said.

Erin's almost to the point of one hundred days past her transplant. "A hundred days is a very important time," she told me. "It means I can have one friend over and I can have fast food and I can have things like raw tomatoes and carrots." In other words, it will be time to take little risks with the world of germs.

This was the first day Erin climbed onto my lap – once while I sat in a chair and once on the floor. When we sat together on the floor, Annie climbed into Erin's lap. We three held each other and swayed from side to side, singing a song that Erin's classmates have also learned: "We care for each other."

When we studied bones, Erin wanted to know where the liver was because a boy she knows "has trouble with his liver and his eyes got yellow but now his eyes are better and he's doing okay." Monday she told me they sent her friend Brian home because there was no more they could do for him. "So we'll see," she said. But Wednesday when we prayed together, her prayer was, "Jesus, please let Brian have a good time with you up in heaven."

Erin takes most of her innumerable medicines willingly but laughed and showed me her hiding places for the hated vitamins and "poopie pills."

She seems to get along well with her mother, but becomes impatient when Mary Lou insists she keep drinking fluids. Mary Lou has to somehow tread a middle ground between mother and nurse; that must be as hard as trying to teach your own kid piano.

I asked Erin if she'd mind me writing about her. She said I could write about our home-schooling without stressing the medical details. I hope I've done that here. It was clear from what she said that she wants to be looked at as a normal child. I'm a lucky teach. I knew when I took this job that Erin would teach me more than I could teach her.

I've learned about the privilege of the ordinary, being someone who doesn't stand out, being able to go to school.

I've learned about the joy of learning that springs from natural curiosity.

Most important, I've learned about trust, humor and optimism ... and about cheering on a young friend, climb or slide.

[1992]

The sacred duty of parents: nurture the family soul.

Thank You

Sometimes we say thank you without realizing it. So it was with my son and my brother, two young men who nearly drowned.

The first near-drowning happened in 1980 on a hot September day in Florida. It was my brother David's wedding day.

After David and Laura got married under a banyan tree, we gathered around a hotel pool to celebrate. A few wedding guests, including my two little boys and me, changed clothes and jumped into the water to cool off. Some distance away, my husband talked with friends. I put our four-year-old son Charlie in the care of a friend and a relative. Then I sat in the shallow end with our two-year-old son Brian.

I was watching Brian ploch-ploch in the water when suddenly I looked up to see Charlie being dragged out of the water. His arms flapped limp and lifeless across his body. His legs dragged. His whole body was blue, the same color as his eyes ... but his eyes were closed.

I snatched Brian out of the water, shoved him into the arms of the nearest adult, and dashed to where Charlie lay unconscious on the pool's concrete apron. I knelt helplessly at his feet. Somewhere I had learned what to do in emergencies like this, but my memory blurred. I couldn't think.

Nancy, the wedding guest who had spotted Charlie foundering in the water, searched for his pulse, and found none. She breathed into his mouth. My brother, the groom in his white suit, knelt and pressed gently on Charlie's upper body.

The fifteen people who had created a celebratory chatter only moments before now watched from a hushed distance.

The air was sick with fear.

I prayed with no words.

After the longest minute of my life, Charlie's eyelids fluttered; his irises were rolled back into his head. Then he yelped in pain and started coughing: the best sounds I've ever heard – agonized, but full of life. Later he vomited water profusely and spent several days in the hospital with water in his lungs (he had a ball making the bed's head and foot go up and down).

Five years passed, and when Charlie turned nine, I sent a hundred-dollar check to Nancy, with a note that read, "It's Charlie's birthday. If it weren't for you, we might not have had him around during these past years. Thank you."

I never really thanked my brother David for his actions that helped revive Charlie. He probably didn't know what he was doing, but at least he didn't sit there numbly like I did. I understand now that simply jostling an unconscious person and talking to him is better than doing nothing.

I believe that Nancy and David had a hand in giving my son a chance to grow up – and growing up hasn't been easy for him. Like many young people, Charlie went through some very rough spots during his adolescence. But he came through. He's eighteen now, a gentle young man, starting college.

The second near-drowning was less sudden than Charlie's. It involved my brother David and took place gradually over the past sixteen years. David went through some very rough spots as a husband and young father in Florida. He fell in love with the bottle, and he forgot he had family back in Wisconsin. He lost his wife and his home. He nearly didn't make it. But he came through.

As I write this, David is living with my family after going through residential treatment in Milwaukee. He's been sober since August 22, the sixteenth anniversary of the car accident that killed our parents and younger brother. I think those deaths in 1978 helped David (then eighteen) to crawl into the bottle. Nobody suggested grief counseling to my siblings and me back then.

Charlie still lives at home with us. He and David often sit up late, talking. When David lived in the rehab community, Charlie made a point to drive down to see him. Later David told me, "It was really something having Charlie come visit me all by himself. It was like having a new best friend."

Charlie has no memory of David, a young groom full of hopes, leaning over him and pressing on his lungs that day in 1980. I've never mentioned it. Maybe their new friendship is life's way of letting Charlie say thank you. David acted instinctively at the poolside, and his actions helped save Charlie's life. Charlie has acted instinctively in offering David his friendship. A friendship can help save a life, too.

For a short time, Charlie experienced physical pain as he recovered from near-drowning. But the agony was full of life. I'm sure there is suffering in David's long-delayed grief work. No longer does he have alcohol to medicate his feelings away. But his agony is full of life. And he has another chance – for himself and for his children.

Charlie is a college freshman. David is looking for a new job in a new city. Thus each of them begins a new phase of life, full of hopes. And for that I am thankful, thankful.

[1995]

In the days before bike helmets, I set my little brother David into the wire basket mounted on my bicycle handlebars. I gave him rides on the sidewalks of Beckett and Glendale Avenues in Milwaukee. We only wiped out a couple of times.

Going for the Gold

"I heard about it but I haven't seen it," I told Terre. Her eyes grew big as I continued: "It's true. I've used it. Can you believe it? They can put a man on the moon and they can make colored duct tape. Colored duct tape – in our lifetime!"

It's a special friend who understands my love of duct tape. Terre Woodward is one of those, even if I see her only about once a year. But it's true: when we get together with an old friend, it always feels like we said goodbye only yesterday. All the private jokes and ancient stories tumble out of the rusty file cabinets in our brains. And we laugh.

Terre and I have known each other for twenty years. We met when we were neighbors on Plainview Road in the rural Town of Lisbon. It was 1976 and our nation was celebrating its bicentennial; our firstborn sons were in diapers. Both those boys are young men now. Her Ben got married in August, and my Charlie moved away from home that same month, into his first apartment and his first venture into self-support.

We talked about how our sons have yet to learn to "live poor." Terre said Ben's wife puts a brake on his spending. I complained that Charlie buys compact discs and French Roast coffee instead of the cheap kind. "Heck, we used to recycle our coffee grounds!" I said.

"We did? I don't remember that!" Terre said.

"We did. We re-used grounds and added a little fresh." How could she not remember?

There were other things, though, that neither of us could forget....

We used cloth diapers and hung them on the line to dry.

We talked for hours at the kitchen table while our kids played at our feet. While we talked, we worked play-dough with our fingers, over and over, like worry beads.

We made our own play-dough. We made our own yogurt. We dried fruit. We canned hundreds of jars of homegrown produce. We helped each other paint our old clapboard houses.

I call her Terrence. She calls me Gilford.

And together we made a Christmas baby. Yep, my husband and I and Terre's husband helped cause Terre's second son to be born on Christmas Eve of 1978, although Terre wasn't "due" until sometime after Christmas. Charlie and Ben were playing on the floor, my baby Brian was in my arms, and the four of us adults were sitting around and talking at Terre's house.

For some reason, we started playing with "robot hand," the toy that had become part of our Christmas that year. It was a device designed with a long plastic stick that had a mechanical hand at one end and a handle at the other. When you squeezed the handle, the hand suddenly made a gripping motion.

Terre's husband became the master of robot hand. He stuck the stick up his sleeve and made the robot hand move as if on its own. He added appropriate dialog. We almost fell off our chairs laughing. Belly laughing.

Terre laughed herself right into the delivery room.

I remember an old Girl Scout song that goes "Make new friends, but keep the old. One is silver and the other gold." I think old friends are gold.

Even if they don't remember recycling coffee grounds.

[1996]

43

Anna and Her Chickens

A chicken is not a loveable creature,
with sharp claws and beak, raspy voice and stink.
How much love inside my Anna Rose,
that she loved her chickens so.

[2006]

Anna and Goldie, 1987

Busha

I spot Busha right away. Her white hair is like a beacon in a sea of grey. The hair is straight, thick, boyish. Busha sits, hunched over, alone, at the dining table in the corner. As I walk toward her, I see that she is poking with her fork at a mound of mashed potatoes.

It's my first time seeing Busha in a nursing home. Over the past couple of years, I have visited her in other places: first her granddaughter's home in Menomonee Falls, then a group home in Brookfield, most recently her daughter's apartment in Germantown.

(Before meeting her, I never heard of the name "Busha." Her granddaughter tells me that it's a version of the Polish word for grandmother, commonly spelled "Busia." It's pronounced "Boosha" and the family spells it simply Busha.)

Busha is ninety-four, and she was energetic and alert until recently. Alzheimer's has aged her like a bad miracle and made it impossible for relatives to care for her.

Busha thinks she's in jail. With a stutter she's fallen into lately, she tells me, "They picked me up off the street. Why am I here? I haven't done nothing wrong. Not a thing wrong." I try to explain, but five minutes later she asks the same question. Finally I give up on logic and go for distraction, that technique that used to work for my children. I take her to her room and suggest praying. We say the "Our Father" aloud. Her voice is strong and clear. The stutter is gone. But soon her prayers turn into laments: "Oh God, why me? Oh Jesus, have mercy on me."

I take her on an art tour. I push her wheelchair out of her room and proceed slowly through the halls, pointing out every picture: images of peach blossoms, picket fences, dogwood, lilacs.

"They're lovely," Busha says. She smiles. Then she sees a picture of a little girl wearing long black stockings and a bonnet.

"Did you wear those?" I ask.

"Oh, yes," she answers. Her voice is prim, delighted – the sound of a mature woman remembering. The "Oh God, why me" voice has disappeared. This is the Busha I remember best. It is how she spoke when she narrated her memories and I wrote them down, before she got so bad.

I wheel her back to her room. She can't hear much out of her left ear, even with the hearing aid, so I switch to her right side. I sing straight into her ear, every old song I can think of: "I only want a buddy, not a sweetheart" (Pop used to sing that); "America the beautiful"; "You are my sunshine"; "Come, Holy Ghost."

Finally I sing "Take me out to the ball game." Her body sways with my singing. The side of my forehead touches the side of her forehead. I can see her trembling lips moving slightly with the words as I sing them.

"We used to go to the ball game all the time on ladies' night, my sister-in-law and me," she says. Her voice is warm. I know she is remembering her days in the Polish neighborhood surrounding St. Mary of Czestochowa in Milwaukee.

"Were you a party girl, Busha?"

"Yes, a little bit."

"That's okay."

"Not any more. I'm too tired."

Soon I say goodbye. Before I leave, Busha asks, "Will you watch over me?"

"Yes," I tell her.

[2000]

Edie

I met her in 1981, when I moved to Menomonee Falls, two doors down the road from her home. She was a youngish old lady then, and she has stayed a youngish old lady for the twenty-three years that I've known her and her husband, George, who is a youngish old man.

Her name was Edith Schneider, and she was the neighbor you wish you had: never nosy, always cheerful, always glad, and pleasantly surprised, to see you.

Edie and George were a quiet institution in Menomonee Falls. They spent many years delivering alert systems to senior citizens. They installed the systems and explained their use. Often I'd see them on their way to an alert system call, wearing identical biker jackets, zooming along on their big touring Harley, tall George in front, tiny Edie in back.

My kids soon learned that Edie was the architect of what she called aggravation cookies – cookies so delicious it was an aggravation to stop eating them. There were always cookies on hand, fresh or in the freezer. (Edie never could have kept her slim shape had she gobbled them all down herself.) Those cookies inspired my children to make many surprise visits to Edie.

Sometimes my husband and I would wander across the back yards on a sultry evening to visit George and Edie when we'd see them out burning brush. We'd stand close to the fire to avoid the mosquitoes, talking and laughing about nothing important. No matter where or when I caught Edie, her hair was always done just-so and her nails polished beautifully.

Edie and George shared the work of a large garden and a huge yard. I often saw her hauling water to the vegetables, in watering cans. My most vivid picture of Edie, however, is that little lady pushing a lawn mower. George would be cutting grass rows with his vintage tractor while Edie did trim work. She was still pushing that mower last summer, when she was eighty-seven years old.

She fought cancer on and off for the past few years. She put up with more obnoxious treatments and their aftermath than I think I would have had the guts to do. She was not ready to leave.

But she left, finally. She took one last look at all the flowers in her yard, went inside, shut her eyes, and was gone the next day. It was June 6, the day after her and George's 67th wedding anniversary. She left, I know she had to leave, but I'm sure going to miss her. And oh, what will George do without his Edie?

[2004]

Edie and George Schneider were German-Americans, like many Wisconsinites. My mother, a farmer's daughter from St. Michael's, Wisconsin, used German words to refer to household objects. I continue her tradition (although I have no idea how to spell the words). A potato masher is always a "schtumpfer." When our son Charlie lived in his first apartment and his apartment mates wanted to mash spuds, Charlie said, "Do we have a schtumpfer?" The roomies looked at him like he was crazy.

Uncle Ray

Ray Casey was the city cousin. Audrey Hoerig, my mother, was the country cousin. They grew up as close as brother and sister even though he lived in Milwaukee and she lived more than an hour away on a dairy farm in tiny St. Michael's.

Their closeness grew after their marriages, because they and their spouses all liked each other – a magical thing never guaranteed to happen in any family. Thus Ray became Uncle Ray to me, someone much more important than "my mother's cousin."

I can see him with absolute clarity, a tall lanky guy with a shock of straight dark hair falling across his forehead, blue eyes alight, sly smile, head ducking down after making a goofy joke.

When my brothers and sister and I were growing up, we often visited at Uncle Ray's house. Sometimes we went there on a weekday and Mum played cards with Uncle Ray's wife, Vi (never "Aunt Vi," I don't know why). Sometimes we drove to see them on a weekend, when Pop and Uncle Ray could be there too.

In the 1950s, Ray and Vi lived in Milwaukee, like we did. When Ray and Vi came to visit, it was always cards, cigarettes, laughter, and Brach's bridge mix. We kids loved getting up the next morning and eating the leftover chocolate covered nuts and raisins.

Uncle Ray's family was growing, and so was ours. There were plenty of us cousins to play together, and neighbor kids, too. When we visited the Casey household, we did a lot of running between their duplex and the one next door. It was dark between the two tall houses – I felt a little spooked. The duplexes were so close that the sun never shone there.

Ray and Vi's kids had a toy that I loved: a big punching bag in the shape of a clown. The clown was about as tall as I was. It had a weighted round bottom. We punched it and it popped right back again. I always wanted one of those.

Eventually the Caseys became the country cousins. They moved to an old farmhouse on Shady Lane in Menomonee Falls, and we stayed in our Cape Cod in Milwaukee. Our families kept growing until each had three boys and two girls, arranged in almost perfect age-steps mirroring each other.

Uncle Ray's farmhouse was a place of fascination to me. It had an enclosed sun porch jutting out the front, where Uncle Ray did his painting. I liked to be in that room; it seemed secret. Once he and I were in the sun porch together and Uncle Ray showed me a painting he had made of Vi. He loved that picture. He talked to me about the picture for a long time, and as young as I was, I figured out that he was really talking to me more about Vi and not so much about his art.

The farmhouse had an upstairs with vents in the floor. We kids could open the vents to get heat from the first floor – and to spy on anyone below, a wonderful thing. Boy, did we giggle at the adults beneath us. We were sure they had no idea about our covert activities.

Ray and Vi's farmhouse had a dining room, exotic to me. In the dining room was a hutch and on the hutch was a coffee grinder you had to operate by hand. I marveled at that grinder, although I didn't understand it. I had never seen a coffee bean.

Outside in the farmyard there stood a Quonset hut that I never went into, and a huge old barn that was a world in itself. We kids wandered around the barn, all cobwebs and dust motes floating in shafts of sunlight. I always had a slight (thrilling) feeling of danger in there. The Casey farmstead included a series of Irish Setters of no great intelligence but great beauty – Uncle Ray laughed at them and loved them. There was a small marshy area near the house that stayed a small marshy area. I liked that spot.

Beyond the farmyard was open land where we kids ran, farm fields all around us, a few houses here and there. In the summer, the humming of heat bugs rang loud in our ears and everywhere around us. Once we cousins walked on Shady Lane up the hill to a neighbor's house, where we took turns with the neighbor kid jumping off the top of the garage lean-to, right down to the ground below. Uncle Ray and the other adults were indoors, playing cards as usual. Children were used to freedom in those days.

Back in the farmhouse, whenever I talked to him, it seemed that Uncle Ray lived to make me laugh. When I was in his presence, I had his complete attention. That is special for a child – for an adult to be truly *present*. I never felt that Uncle Ray was in a hurry to get away from me and return to the adults. He taught me lots of things.

He taught me to love fables. He shared with me a book of Uncle Remus tales. It was an oversized book with a shiny cover, produced by Disney after its Uncle Remus animated movie. It didn't matter if the day was sunny or rainy – every time we visited the farmhouse, my first stop was the couch with the big Uncle Remus book propped on my lap. I gobbled up every story of the always-clever Brer Rabbit, a small creature who had his share of troubles yet consistently outwitted Brer Fox and avoided becoming stew. "Born and bred in a briar patch" – that cracked me up.

Uncle Ray taught me about art. He had graduated from Layton School of Art and was employed as an artist for *The Milwaukee Sentinel*. He found out I liked to do cartooning and drawing in general.

"Draw me something," he said one day.

Somehow I flung off my flowing cape of self-consciousness and managed to sketch a figure of a girl. My fingers felt as trembly as they did when people asked me to play a tune on the piano.

"Here, I'll show you how to do body proportion," he said. He demonstrated that my girl was much too short. "You can measure figures by heads," he explained. "A baby is three heads tall. A child is four heads tall. An adult is seven or eight heads tall." He re-drew my figure and I saw the improvement.

Uncle Ray taught me about body language one day when he noticed me touching my nose as I entered a room. "You can always tell when someone's self-conscious because they'll scratch their nose or touch their face some way," he said. That was a strong lesson for a young learner.

One day, when I was much older, we had a long, serious talk about alcoholism and about how husbands should treat their wives. Uncle Ray had seen a lot during his life. I have never forgotten the things he told me.

Visiting Uncle Ray's farmhouse all those years must have influenced me. "Country" became stamped on my heart, although I never lived in the country during my growing years. When I became a married woman, country was the place I wanted to be.

Mike and I moved to a house with a barn and ten acres on Custer Lane in Menomonee Falls. Custer Lane used to be part of Shady Lane. It's down the road and around a sharp corner from Uncle Ray's old farmhouse. I was amazed when I discovered the house right there where it should be, even though he and Vi had moved away, to Sussex, long before.

The big barn and Quonset hut are gone, but the marshy area is still a marshy area, and the enclosed sun porch still juts out proudly from the front. The home is surrounded by subdivisions, with patches of marsh and field nearby. I've passed by the farmhouse countless times on my bike, always tempted to knock on the door and talk to the folks who live there now. I bet kids still spy on adults through the floor vents. It wouldn't be the same place, though, without the hutch and the coffee grinder and the Uncle Remus book.

Most of all, it wouldn't be the same without Uncle Ray.

During my adult years, I got to know Uncle Ray in a different way. His string-bean frame filled out, and his dark hair grew white. Yet the sparkle still danced in his eyes, and he still ducked his head after a goofy joke. He remained tall, though somewhat stooped, and always ready to laugh.

We became colleagues at Waukesha County Technical College. He taught water color painting and I taught creative writing. My sister Sally taught math there, and all of us would get together with our spouses at the college's annual dinners. It was there that I told him I had become a grandmother. Uncle Ray said he was envious, because all his grandchildren were grown up. He said, "There's nothing like a little one."

I enjoyed asking him questions that never would have occurred to me to ask before. I questioned him about my dad, long gone. Uncle Ray always spoke of Pop in the fondest way, referring to him as "Red" or "the Irishman." Ray and his sister, my Aunt Shirley, enjoyed the fact that Pop was half-Irish, like they were. The more I talked to Uncle Ray, the more it became apparent that he and Pop shared many secrets that I would never know. All I could be sure of was that the secrets were funny.

As a married woman, I saw Uncle Ray in a different light: as a married man. When I visited him and Vi, I found them to be a most loving – and ever-arguing – couple. He'd speak and she'd correct him, or she'd speak and he'd correct her. They argued, they smiled, and they so obviously loved each other that the arguing was funny. They both had the driest of dry senses of humor, which gave perspective to everything.

In his later years, Uncle Ray experienced serious physical problems. At one point he became so ill that he lost a great deal of weight, proving his assertion that "you should always keep a little extra weight in case you get sick."

Eventually Uncle Ray experienced great depression. He gave up teaching and painting. When I saw him at our summer family reunions, I saw only an occasional flicker of the sparkle that had once danced in his blue eyes. The sparkle may have been gone, but the love never disappeared. I still felt that love when I sat to talk with him.

Vi told me they had explored every avenue but could find no cure for Uncle Ray's depression. I thought it especially cruel that depression cloaked the man who had lived to make others laugh. I know Uncle Ray's depression was hard for Vi to deal with. Yet when I spoke with her, she didn't complain. She loved the man and felt only compassion for his suffering.

Before his depression set in, Uncle Ray decided to leave a legacy to his family: his art. He started distributing a print of one of his paintings. It's an abstract study of a waterfall with seagulls, in purples and greens.

"How did you do it? From a photograph?" I asked him.

"I saw the waterfall and painted it from memory," he told me.

My print is number forty-six of five hundred.

"I gave your sister Sally a lower number, because she's my godchild," Uncle Ray explained, sheepish grin on his face.

I had the print framed. It's the focal point behind my living room couch. I was proud to show it to Uncle Ray last time he visited my house, during the summer of 2005.

How wonderful to be able to leave art for your family. Uncle Ray died today, and all I can leave for him is a little tribute in words.

Yet he and I knew the best gift, something we can all give any time: love.

[2006]

It's too bad I learned the word "Ach!" at a young age. My mother and grandmother said it with a great deal of spittle. The word "Ach!" has been the end of many a weight-loss plan for me.

Dorothy

Dorothy was probably the skinniest person I've ever known, and the most feisty. Genghis Khan would have loved to have her in his cavalry. I can picture Dorothy riding the lightest horse, her long thin arms and legs dangling in a pencil-thin suit of armor. And the enemy would *run scared.*

Our friend Maxine called yesterday and told me that Dorothy died. I felt sad, but not shocked. I had known for about a month that Dorothy was in the hospital. When I found out, I taped a note to my kitchen cabinet. It read simply, "Dorothy." That was my reminder to visit or call, send flowers or at least send a card.

I never got around to visiting or calling or sending my good wishes. First I was out of town and after that I got too darn wrapped up in busy-ness – and of course I *knew* Dorothy would get well again. Dorothy always got well again – because she was such a fighter.

When I learned she died, I was immediately filled with guilt. Why hadn't I made time to let her know how much I cared? Then I remembered that at least I prayed for her. And I believe wherever she is now, she understands all. I'm guessing I'm forgiven.

I saw her in July, right before her latest bout with ill health. I had called her to do a volunteer project at HOPE Network for Single Mothers, the nonprofit agency where I'm employed. We worked together for a couple of hours, and we were quickly back to our old ways: laughing at the world and at each other. That was always how it was with us. Dorothy and I were never bosom buddies, but we had a mutual admiration that expressed itself in sarcasm.

Dorothy, you see, wasn't that stereotyped friend that movies love to portray: the sweet woman dying young, bravely suffering, spouting wisdom and spreading love. Dorothy drank. She smoked. In private conversation with a friend, she used colorful language when it fit the subject. Yes, she did die young. Yes, she did suffer bravely. But when Dorothy spouted wisdom, it came on the tip of a sharp tongue. And she did indeed spread love, but it was tough love on her terms. Curmudgeon love.

Ask any kid who went to St. Mary's school for a quotation from her. The answer will be: "Tuck in your shirt!" She took uniforms seriously. Many teachers become blasé, but not Dorothy. Even after she had taught for decades, even when she was struggling with painful illnesses, she never let up on those kids. *Tuck in your shirt,* darn it! She nagged because she cared. She never gave up. She never quit fighting.

When I had substitute teacher duty at St. Mary's, I'd often get a little care package from Dorothy sent via a student: coffee candy full of caffeine to buck me up. Or she might send me a cup of coffee. Now *that* was love.

She had become diabetic as a teen, and was told she wouldn't live past age thirty or so. Boy, did she prove them wrong. She lasted until age fifty-eight.

Dorothy had a brittle diabetes that affected her vision. It got to the point she couldn't drive at night, which made it hard for her on nights when there were parent-teacher conferences at school.

Because of her medical condition, Dorothy was never able to bear children. But that didn't stop her. She became a mother to several children who needed an "alternate" mother because of problems large and small. With those children came the difficulties – and joys – experienced by parents everywhere.

Dorothy really knew kids – through teaching and through nurturing them at home. When we worked together last July, Dorothy told me her first "grandchild" was soon to be born. She was as thrilled as any blood grandma.

And then there is Jim. Dorothy and Jim married sometime in the 1970s, around when Mike and I married. That means they were wed for more than three decades. Like all marriages, theirs was not without its rocks and bumps. But they stuck, taking turns helping each other. They shared a creative vision and had the most beautiful back yard I've ever seen, filled with twisty paths and bridges and exotic-looking plants. And they loved their dogs.

I asked Maxine about Jim. She said he's having a rough time. He's hardly been at work this last month because he's been so attentive to Dorothy. You hear about spouses who fall apart with their loved one dies, because they've lost a job: the job of caring for someone. Jim is the one who needs our prayers now.

About seven years ago, Dorothy had a kidney and pancreas transplant. Before that she had been performing dialysis during breaks from teaching, in a little private room at school. I don't know how she had the strength to drag herself there. And she taught junior high age kids, not the easiest group. The transplanted pancreas failed her, so her diabetes remained. But the kidney lasted and gave her these last years when she could enjoy a bit of retirement.

Then in August they discovered she had colon cancer. Time for a colostomy bag. Maxine told me that was the beginning of the end of Dorothy's fighting. How can you go four decades with one physical battle after another? How do you keep your spirits up when you rarely feel good?

I don't blame Dorothy for easing up. It's hard enough to fight the world when you're well. How do you fight when you're ill? Dorothy's sarcasm was probably her best armor in struggles harder than Genghis Khan ever knew.

Last weekend, Dorothy had a heart attack. Her body couldn't take it anymore.

"She must have weighed about eighty pounds," Maxine told me.

"Was she ready to go see God?" I asked.

"Yes. She just wanted to sleep."

She lived about a day after the heart attack. She knew it was over. Even for a warrior like Dorothy, the battle had come to an end.

"I picture her in heaven with a light beautiful body," I told Maxine.

"Yeah, and no waiting for her. She gets skips."

Take skips? Probably. Shirt tucked in? Definitely. And no more need for armor.

[2006]

When times get tough, you learn how much of a fighter you are.

Recapitating St. Francis

It always happens that something I love gets broken.
So it was with St. Francis.

I had wanted one for years,
and finally our daughter Anna made me a
ceramic St. Francis with a wolf and two birds.
She glazed them all in glossy pewter, like shiny metal.

An hour after I set St. Francis outside, Mike knocked
him over,
breaking off half an arm –
so many pieces, impossible to glue.
Yet I kept St. Francis in our rock garden,
jagged arm stump jutting,
rationalizing: the break is symbolic –
we must be the arm of St. Francis.

(Mike said the wolf bit off the arm and
we should paint the edge red.
I said no.)

For years the one-armed St. Francis stood amid
grape hyacinths or impatiens.
In time, both birds fell off and
only the wolf remained his companion.
Then last week Mike toppled him again.
This time when St. Francis fell, his head broke off.

For a couple of weeks, the saint's body lay in the dirt
near his rolled-away head,
until a friend visited and noticed,
and I was ashamed enough to grab
St. Francis and his head
and bring them into the house.

Last night I said to Mike, "Do you want to recapitate
St. Francis?"
Mike said sure. So I got the Krazy Glue
and ran to the basement to fetch the de-antlered buck
that Brian, our son, made so long ago,
carefully glazed to look real.
The buck's place was my flower bed,
but somehow he too got broken.
I couldn't display him that way,
and I hate to glue things,
so for years the deer remained on my laundry table,
his fawn beside him.

"Can you glue this too?" I asked Mike,
holding out a hand full of ear and antler pieces.
"Sure," he said.
"I'll help," I told him,
hoping he wouldn't need me,
because I don't like to glue things.

But I did hold pieces together after Mike glued them.
While they dried, we talked about how
he made models when he was a boy.
He used rubber bands to hold pieces together,
or held them with his fingers,
reading assembly directions while the glue dried.

I thought about my dad telling me how
when he was a boy
he walked around town so he could listen to his
corduroy knickers rub together.
He called them "whistle britches" because they
squeaked like a whistle.

Kids used to have a lot of patience, I thought.
Kids entertained themselves.

Then I realized I had glued my fingers together
with the Krazy Glue.
Mike pulled them apart without blood, but
it hurt and left a horrible glue residue
like dead skin.
I said, "I should stay away from glue."

Today, for some reason,
I worked by myself on the buck
and didn't glue my fingers together,
but soon realized we're missing one whole antler.
After all our work,
the buck might have to resume laundry duty.
I can't rationalize a one-antler buck in the flower bed,
even though antlers drop off in real life –
it just looks odd.

St. Francis was fine this morning, totally recapitated.
I used a black marker to color the white chips
on his forehead and cowl.
After wrestling all the ear and antler pieces,
I was glad St. Francis had only one head
and it was in one piece.

I might hang a little flower basket on his half-arm to
hide the jagged edge;
I bet the real St. Francis liked flowers.

Normally I don't like lawn knick-knacks,
and I hate gluing,
but Anna made St. Francis when she was a little girl
and Brian made the buck when he was a little boy.

[2007]

No one "has" time. We make time.

Mother to My Mother Figure

Nancy Reinsvold is my friend. Her doc told her that she'd be dead by July ... in 2011. It's 2012 now, and she's still here.

She's almost seventy-eight, and she's been fighting pancreatic cancer for nearly five years. I visited her at her home in Menomonee Falls today, as I do every week, and we sat on the couch laughing about this and that. Her hardest laugh came when she told me about a robber who drove his car through the glass windows of an Apple store, in order to steal a bunch of computers. Unknown to him, the license plate fell off his car in the process. The police were waiting for him when he got back home.

Boy, did Nancy laugh. I could see all her teeth.

I gave her a photo I took of her. "I look so old," she complained.

"You earned all those wrinkles," I countered.

She would have none of it.

I love the picture. It shows her holding a cigarette. When she got diagnosed with cancer, she quit smoking. She chewed a lot of nicotine gum. Now she's back to the smokes, big giant boxes of them that her son buys for her at a discount. I think how stale they must get. But they're cheap.

In the photo I took of her, Nancy holds a giant tomato in her lap – one she grew. She was so proud of it. She invited me over when the tomato was ripe, because she knows I love bacon-lettuce-tomato sandwiches. I cut up the giant tomato into thick wedges, and we had a BLT feast.

She undergoes chemotherapy from time to time – not as often as her doc wants, but all she can stand. She has trouble keeping food down, and not only because of the chemo. She doesn't know what makes her nauseated. It disgusts her. When she gains weight, she's happy, but she mostly loses weight. To be gentle on her stomach, she eats soft foods. She is sick of Ensure and oatmeal and yogurt and pudding. She's down to 100 pounds and wears a size zero jeans.

She told me the story of how her pants fell off her the other day. Her arms were laden with a case of non-alcoholic beers her son had given her, and all of a sudden she realized her pants were around her ankles. She couldn't pull them up because her hands were full, so she looked back at her son and said, "I'm mooning you."

She added that the trousers that fell down were the pants I hate: the red ones with the manufactured worn-out look – a tear here, a tear there, all threadbare. I can't believe she wears them, but she loves 'em. I laughed and said I wish they'd melt away entirely.

She toils in her vegetable and flower gardens. Many times when I visit, her jeans have dirt-covered knees. She told me she worked so hard the other day that she had to come in and rest. She had already put in hours of labor. It was 8:00 a.m.

"That's probably why you're still alive. You work," I told her.

"Yeah," she said.

She tried to move a heavy lawn ornament in spring. It fell on her and afterward, her side hurt a lot. Three months later, the doc looked at an MRI and said, "You broke your rib." But he said it had healed well.

"You've got cancer but you still mend well. It's amazing," I said.

She agreed.

We talked about some serious stuff like terrorists and weather disasters. She said, "I don't know what's gonna happen to our world. The killing and the taking God off our money and the hurricanes and the drought." When I have insomnia, these are some of the thoughts of my dark nights of the soul. Nancy and I don't talk about these things often. More commonly we complain about silly stuff, like about people who talk all the time, people who interrupt. Nancy talks nice and slow, the way I like. I keep trying to do the same.

Today she reminisced about being a single mother to three young boys, working on the assembly line at the Briggs & Stratton factory full-time for thirty-eight years to keep a roof over their heads, never having a car. "I had to take my baby in a stroller through the snow to the babysitter at 4:00 a.m.," she said. "I don't know how I did it ... you do what you have to do."

Nancy's husband had abandoned her when they had two young sons and she was pregnant with their third. She has always had a heart for single mothers. I met her when she became a volunteer for the charity I founded, HOPE Network for Single Mothers. She was a hilarious volunteer, part of a team that sorted and folded donated clothing. She was the one to put funny hats on her head or drape silly-looking dresses over her own clothing. Always the clown. She confessed that she took some HOPE clothing home to give to Eric, her garbage man. His daughter is a single mom. I told her that was fine.

That's the kind of person Nancy is. Her recipe for survival is simpler than what we find in a lot of self-help books: Laugh. Laugh at yourself. Volunteer. Work hard. Get dirty. Give stuff away. Don't be afraid to ask for help. Reach out to your neighbors (the garbage man too). And don't give up.

She volunteered for a lot of other charities – all without having a car. President Bush sent her a commendation for her volunteerism. It hangs in a frame on her wall.

She talked about her sons, all grown men now, with families. She appreciates the work they do for her. But most of all, she appreciates when they *visit*.

I started visiting Nancy back when she began fighting the cancer. I usually bring soup. When I started my visits, it was from a feeling of appreciation. I was grateful to Nancy for all the time she had given to my charity. But over the years, something changed. My feeling of appreciation turned into *love*. I don't know how my feeling changed, or where it changed, or even why. It just did. Nancy and I say "I love you" every time we talk. She calls me "Sweetheart." I call her "Sweetie pie." She gives me smooches right on the lips and I hug her skinny bones.

My mother died in 1978. I had to raise my children without her guidance and love. That was hard. Nancy is almost 78, just a bit younger than my own mom would be if she were alive. Nancy is a friend to me, and I've imagined her as a kind of mother.

That's what I *thought*, anyway.

I have known for a long time that Nancy's mother died when Nancy was a baby. In all her years, she has never known a mother's love. She raised her three sons without the support of a partner or a mom. She told me that she finds some comfort in the thought that she'll finally meet her mother after she leaves this earth.

The other day Nancy told me something that shocked me. Her wrinkly face burst into more wrinkles when she smiled and said, "I tell my son that you're my mother."

She started calling me Mother Dear.

But I fooled her. I call her Mother Dear too.

[2012]

Through volunteering with HOPE Network, I've come to know many women in the Greater Milwaukee area who are raising children on their own. Single mothers are the most resourceful people I've ever met.

Part Three
Living the Seasons

A squirrel taking a nap in my yard one spring day

April 3, Still the Unlocking

She realized
that the unlocking was almost over
when the goldfinches got their gold back on
and her skies awoke with sandhill cranes,
redwing blackbirds, robins,
and her most beloved,
the great blue heron.

Yet the juncos, her snow angels,
remained, grey and white,
so she knew the unlocking
held its grey grip
and true spring, all blue and yellow,
had not arrived.

And she sighed, dreamed of azaleas
purple, pink and white,
in the land of her birth,
dreamed of living
where the mockingbird lives.

[2003]

Years ago, Kurt Vonnegut spoke at the University of Wisconsin-Waukesha "Wilderness University" series. He said that in the North, we have six seasons: summer, fall, the locking, winter, the unlocking, and spring. Thinking about the unlocking helps when "winter" seems to drag on interminably.

Spring Peepers

Every spring for years, I listened to the sound, puzzled about its source. During March mornings I heard it through my open window, sounding like birds or crickets – a chorus of loud, insistent chirping.

Someone told me the sound is spring peepers. I looked in a book. Turns out, spring peepers are green frogs so tiny they look like a rubber toy you'd get from a zoo vending machine. They can be as small as a thumb nail.

When I hear them, I know winter is over: glory be! They herald spring and chirp well into summer. Their voices have become my favorite of all sounds.

One day I snuck up on a marshy area brimming with peeping. I crept quietly but the minute I got close, the chorus abruptly halted. I've never seen a peeper in person.

Their shyness only makes their sound sweeter.

[2006]

When I was nine, our family shared a cottage with the LaBonte family way Up North on Lake Superior. The LaBonte kids told a story of digging on the beach and finding an Indian skull. That night I had trouble sleeping. I heard voices: eerie, echoing voices of multitudes. Indian spirits? Or was I sick with fever and delirium? There is no one to ask – I am left with the spooky memory.

Fences

Our dream came true in 1981. We finally built our place out in the country: ten acres in Menomonee Falls. It looked like another dream was going to come true in the summer of 1982. My husband, Mike, and I were outside with our two little boys when a stranger pulled into the driveway and walked into our back yard.

He said, "I was driving by and noticed that you have a barn. Would you be interested in boarding my horses?"

Heck yeah, we were interested. The stranger's name was Gene, and we struck a deal with him fast and fair, to our minds. Gene could use our barn and acreage for his three horses for free if he built fences and fed the animals. For no work on our part, we'd have the pleasure of seeing horses "make a landscape look more beautiful," as Alice Walker wrote.

We learned quickly that we should have specified the type of fencing. In my mind, it was going to be white wooden fencing like I'd seen on the horse farms in Kentucky.

What Gene did was string wire from post to post. The posts were about fifty feet apart. If Mike and I hadn't been such city kids, we would have intervened. We learned, the hard way, that wire strung between posts *fifteen* feet apart might have been strong enough to contain three horses.

Other things we learned:

Horses want to break through a fence, no matter how roomy their playground.

Horses will push until they find the weakest part of a fence.

Accidentally touching an electric fence can make a person jump.

Apparently, electricity isn't much of a deterrent to a big horse with his thick winter coat.

When horses get loose and wander to a neighboring church parking lot, the police will be called and Mike will have to retrieve the animals, even if he's already dressed in his suit and tie for work.

Chicken feed in a bucket is like a drug to horses – they'll follow the bucket anywhere, even back home inside their fence.

In 1984, I was five months pregnant with our third child when I found myself wrestling Chief, a palomino quarter horse and the biggest of Gene's three equines. Chief had gotten outside the fence again. He reared up like "Fury" and broke the wagon I had tied him to. Luckily, he didn't hurt me or my unborn daughter.

After that incident, we told Gene it was time for the horses to find a new home. We enjoyed the big animals for the years they lived with us and graced our horizon. We were sad to see them go, but relieved.

Good fences might have made good horses.

[2006]

When we boarded three horses, my Uncle Jerry Hoerig laughed. He and my mother had grown up on a dairy farm in St. Michael's, Wisconsin. He called the horses "hay burners," implying that they were useless. I always thought it was useful to bring beauty to the landscape.

Flood

We are in the full-milk bosom of summer. Nature is full. She bursts in a profusion of blossoms, pungency, heat, and mosquitoes.

I walk on my land in the dark, along deer paths I have mowed wider. Lightning bugs – "fireflies" – illuminate my walk. Beyond the tops of tall bushes, our community hospital looms, remote, like a cobra. Sometimes I feel like a deer blinded by headlights, running in panic.

Who will guard the little bits of wild that we have left?

The rains pour in a torrent. Suddenly, just down the road, the Fox River, usually a sluggish creek, remembers that it is a river. Crayfish swim in my neighbor's driveway-pond after the Fox bursts from its banks.

People forget that nature is boss. They walk without heed across our little neighborhood bridge that has become a mini-Niagara. How easily they might be swept into the woods-now-a-lake.

Drivers plow through the flood in their cars, risking lost brakes.

People build and build and build, squeezing marshes and filling sloughs that would catch floodwaters like basins. One reader wrote to me: "Mother Nature wants her land back, and my money is on her." It's why I feel like a deer in headlights sometimes.

When fireflies light my way, I know it's time for my son Brian's birthday. This year was no different, although it was Brian's first birthday away from home. He turned nineteen on June 28, and he was with his

U.S. Marine compatriots somewhere in the woods north of Camp Pendleton, California.

On Brian's birthday, my husband Mike and I were working together in the house. We decided to hang Brian's high school letter jacket in a hallway outside Brian's old bedroom. I put the jacket on a wooden hanger. It was heavy, laden with medals and pins from wrestling and gymnastics. Mike sunk wall anchors and used a couple of screws to affix a shiny new garment hook to the wall. I lifted the jacket onto the hook.

We both stood there looking at it. Suddenly we were holding each other and crying: another kind of flood.

"Where did the years go?" Mike asked me.

When I walk through firefly-lighted deer paths, I think of Brian.

[1997]

When summer finally comes to Wisconsin, it goes fast. People are afflicted with a combination of weather ecstasy and sheer panic.

Drought

July 5
Already
purple and yellow everywhere

colors of autumn

[2006]

A best smell: sunbaked pine needles.

August

August is a bell tolling fullness and endings.

August is the month when you find a tomato – fat, firm, juicy and *red* – still warm from the sun. August is the month of foundling zucchini left on my doorstep. And, if I don't pick them, apples from my trees start dropping to the ground.

Best of all in August is Wisconsin sweet corn, sold some places (gulp) for three dollars a dozen, and at fairs for three dollars an ear. Yipes! Still, who would put a price tag on ecstasy? Mmmm, so sweet it doesn't need butter and so fresh it won't stick in my teeth. As long as it's picked today, I really don't care what it costs. When else during the whole year do I eat it?

August is usually the month of brown grass, but this year, where I live, the rain won't stop. I like to watch how every year is different and favors different wild plants. Mullein and milkweed are doing well this year. Good for the monarchs.

August sounds are unique. The cricket calls louder than before, not only at night but even during daytime. The cicada's buzz pierces the air. My mother called the cicada the "heat bug." "When the heat bug sings, you know it's at least eighty degrees," she said.

Even without a calendar, I'd know that it's August because of the sharpness of those insect sounds. Is the air more still? More thin? Or perhaps we have more humidity, and sounds travel on the moisture in the air. Maybe that's it, like when you're in a boat, fishing, and you can hear a conversation clear across the lake. August teaches us to watch what we say.

I like to walk at night in August because of the terrific stillness. It's almost as still as in winter, when snow muffles all. When my husband and I walk, we usually don't talk. It would seem a sacrilege to break the silence. During our night walks, we see a few lightning bugs flitting about, the last of the summer.

August is ripe with sights and tastes and sounds, but our eyes tell us summer is ending. Already the grasses, flowers, shrubs, and trees begin to change color. Birds begin to flock and make ready for their big trips. Domestic animals start shedding their summer coats.

Gradual ... all is gradual. I'm so glad I can taste, see, smell, and hear.

[1997]

Coneflowers during August at Little Green Lake

The thing about "Up North" in Wisconsin: nobody agrees where Up North begins. Does it start when the soil changes from clay to sand? Does it begin when the pine trees take over the land? Maybe it commences where folks start talking like Canadians, eh? (If that were true, most of Milwaukee would qualify as Up North.)

After the Heat Wave

Sultry
lovely
seventy degrees
11:15 at night
crickets chirping
raindrops rolling off leaves and
hitting the roof in plops
breeze blowing on my body as I
lie on the bed

Windows open again
finally
after blazing days in the nineties

Is the siege over?
We'll find out tomorrow.

[2006]

My heart sings when I see a great blue heron – and
when I see a hoppy toad the size of my thumb nail.

We Canoed Around the Whole Lake!

My friend Pauline Beck and I talked about it for two years: we were going to canoe the whole perimeter of Little Green Lake.

Every summer for four years, I had suggested this endeavor to my husband, Mike, but he said we couldn't do it.

Pauline and I plotched our paddles around a little bit, two summers ago. Then last summer we waited too long and the season got away from us. This summer we re-scheduled three or four times.

Finally, on Labor Day evening, Pauline drove up to our house trailer on the lake at the same time that Mike drove away from it to go back home to Menomonee Falls. When Pauline arrived, darkness had just fallen. She and I launched immediately into training for the canoe event. This involved us donning tennis shoes and walking to Vandy's bar, where we touched the dumpster (to make the walk count. You must always touch the dumpster to make the walk count). Then we walked back to the trailer. Time: forty minutes. Training fuel: two beers, Leinenkugel's Summer Shandy, I believe.

After a brief talk fest (to keep the jaws limber; athletes must keep limber), Pauline and I repaired to our beds. We slept well.

In the morning, we omitted breakfast because I am paranoid about having to pee. Athletes must make sacrifices. (I had considered wearing Depends, but I nixed that idea.)

We doused ourselves in sunscreen and walked to the point, a natural area beyond the house trailer campground and grassy boat yard.

"Pauline!" I said. Very quietly.

We stopped.

There was a bald eagle perched in a willow straight ahead. We crept silently and slowly, hugging our paddles and life jackets close to our bodies as if to make ourselves look smaller.

The eagle had great shoulders. His big white head was a beacon. The closer we got, the bigger he seemed. We got nearer than I thought we would before finally he swooped away. As he swooped, we saw the great white area on his back and tail.

We walked to where the canoe was hidden in the bushes. It's an old watercraft, probably forty years old. It belonged to my mom and dad, and they died back in 1978. Pop ordered it from L.L. Bean and paid extra for a bow decal of an Indian in a headdress. The make of the craft is Old Town "Chippewayan," if I remember right. Pop was so proud of that canoe. He and Mum took me out for a float in it when I was eight months pregnant with Charlie, my first child. We paddled through a dawn mist on Pewaukee Lake. There was nothing but mist and us. Afterward we went fishing from shore. I had the pleasure of fishing as trains clattered by on tracks along the shore, refreshing a childhood memory of fishing with my pop.

My Uncle Jerry loves to tell the story of when Pop fished from that canoe and hooked a lunker. The canoe tipped, and Pop lost his fishing gear and a brand-new reel. Uncle Jerry still laughs his head off at that memory. Pop never fished from the canoe again, as far as I know.

"We should stretch," I told Pauline. An athlete can't be in a hurry. We moved our arms up and around. We stooped over. We probably looked like two goofs there on the point, but no one was around to see.

By 8:35, we dipped our paddles into the water. I paddled in front, Pauline steered in back. The water was green and scummy, the result of a too-warm summer where the water temperature approached ninety degrees Fahrenheit.

We got as close to the marsh as we could, but because of the scum, we couldn't get near enough to be able to see the amazing emerald-green bullfrog I had spied last summer. We did see a couple of turtle heads pokin' out.

Now we paddled into clearer water. The sun was already hot and we were glad we started as early as we did. We had postponed this outing from a day the week before when the weatherman had predicted ninety-five degrees. Today was supposed to get "only" into the eighties.

I warned Pauline that I was going to paddle slowly, to save myself and my poor old fused neck. An athlete must know her limits. That was fine with Pauline. We didn't promise ourselves anything. What would be would be.

We decided to bypass the little bays, to make it more likely that we would get around the lake. We saw great blue heron after great blue heron – swooping, fishing, lurking. That made me happy. For years, I have considered the great blue to be my personal nature symbol. My friend Arleen told me that some Indian tribe calls them the "sha-sha-ga" – probably for their wings in flight, certainly not for their guttural cry.

We heard – then saw – kingfishers. They sounded like nattering squirrels.

We had no conception of the geography of the lake, no idea of how far was a third of the way, or a half. The first part of our trip was the wild part: one-hundred-foot-high sandstone cliffs and forest, cottages perched on top, with trams to the lake. The sun was hot.

Then we came to a landing and (glory be) a port-a-potty. We pulled to shore and we each took a preventive leak. As General Wellington said, "The first rule of war is to pee when you can." (Or something like that.)

Back in the water, we paddled past a bunch of beautiful lake homes. We saw an eagle (the same one?) again a couple of times, and as many great blue herons as I've seen in the Florida Everglades. Finally we started on the southern shore and could paddle in shade. A mercy.

Suddenly, it seemed, we were at Vandy's bar. Now I knew where I was: very close to our house trailer campground. Mike and I have canoed the short way to this area, many times.

Pauline and I made it back to our launch point at 10:20. The trip had taken one hour and forty-five minutes. Had we canoed the little bays, it probably would have added a half-hour to our trip.

The whole time we paddled, we talked. (Keeping all parts limber.) I found out that Pauline is going to turn sixty in a couple of weeks. She's not going to have a party. "This is your party," I said. "You canoed a whole lake for your sixtieth birthday!" She liked that.

I've got almost two years on Pauline. I felt pretty proud of the feat, myself. I called Mike to tell him the whole lake perimeter *could* be paddled, even by geezers. After Pauline and I nestled the canoe back in the bushes, we stretched some more. An athlete must release the built-up lactic acid from the muscles (or something like that). I took some Advil when we got back in the trailer – for prevention.

Later, Pauline went online and found that Little Green Lake has about four miles of shoreline. An athlete must check stats. "We canoed four miles!" she said. We did it.

[2012]

A best sound: canoe paddle hitting the water.

Broken by the Heat

In September 2003, Mike and I went to *Festivals Acadiens* in Lafayette, Louisiana. Our aim was to spend three days dancing to live Cajun bands. That we did. But we did something more. We sweated.

We sweated like we had never sweated before. We were dancing all day long outdoors, on grass. We couldn't believe the heat. It was eighty-eight degrees Fahrenheit and so humid we could hardly breathe. Still we danced along with hundreds of people old and young who surrounded us in a happy throng.

Then we heard a guy nearby saying, "Thank God the heat broke."

What?

People in Southwest Louisiana know heat like Northerners know snow. It's a way of being broken. You know there's no use fighting it, so you give in. Louisiana folks are as broken by heat in summer as Wisconsin folks are broken by cold in winter. Mike and I have laughed for years about the guy who said "Thank God the heat broke."

Now it's August of 2012, and we're not laughing anymore. This long hot Wisconsin summer isn't even over, and already it's a phenomenon. We're broken. Today it was *only* ninety degrees out. I didn't even run the air conditioner.

Our son, Brian, is on a ten-week duty in Qatar with the Wisconsin Air National Guard's 128th Air Refueling Wing. The other day he said the heat index was one hundred thirty-six degrees. Qatar will break Brian like no Wisconsin summer can do.

[2012]

A best taste: fresh Wisconsin corn on the cob.

It's Kick-Leaf Time!

Recipe for kick-leaf time

Ingredients:
Autumn
You

Directions:
Go outside.
Take a walk.
Kick the leaves in your path.
Listen to the shh-shh-shh.
Smell the heavenly scent.

Servings:
Enjoy as often as possible.

Recommendations:
Thank God for the joy.

[2012]

You know how busy squirrels seem to be? Once I saw a squirrel sleeping on a tree branch. He opened his eyes from time to time. I think he was sun-bathing.

Phantoms

Two days in a row
I smelled it
floating on morning breeze
along the Bugline trail in the forest:
      the scent of a wood fire.

Who would build a campfire
early in the morning
in the middle of nowhere?

I sniffed the air again
and knew that
this was no ordinary
wood fire, aromatic and hearty –

It was even more wonderful,
like sweet grass
burned at a pow wow.
      Are there phantoms in the forest?

[2011]

I wish I sat outdoors more often. The best outdoors-sitter I know is a cigarette lover who won't smoke in her own home. Perhaps I need to take up smoking.

Camping

Silhouettes on canvas walls: leaves blowing in the wind, by moonlight and by sunlight.

Dark nights echoing only the sounds of a cricket cacophony and a distant train whistle.

Scents of a wood campfire in the air, in my clothes, in my hair.

Padding along on a thick pine needle floor, getting lost in the woods, walking around the lake, finding a wildflower I've never seen before, like bottle gentian.

Sleeping whenever I want, however long I want, sleeping deeply.

Listening to bird songs – not to telephones ringing, not to TV/movie/radio noise.

Eating ravenously whenever I'm hungry, the food tasting better than ever because I'm living outside.

Getting gloriously dirty, wearing the same old sweatpants and sweatshirt day and night, forsaking mascara and blow dryers, and loving it.

This is camping.

When people scoff at camping, I understand. I know it's a lot of preparation and trouble to put oneself in a situation of lack of comfort. My friend Mike Nold lives on twenty-five acres in Virginia, and he laughs and says, "Why would I go camping? I live in the woods!"

I live on ten acres of what I consider paradise, too, but still it's not the same as camping. I have to see those leaves on canvas walls. I have to perfume myself with that wood fire.

I'm going camping for four days this week at Pike Lake campground in Hartford, during school break for teacher's convention, with my daughter Anna and her best friend Colleen. I can't wait. I haven't camped for two years, and it's killing me. By the end of our fourth day, I want to be so sick of the smell of wood fire that

I'll be glad to get home again, grateful for my big warm house, and ready to settle in for the winter.

It's hard for us Wisconsin folk to think about winter. I like winter, but I know it gets *looooong*.

That's why we Northerners are ferocious about enjoying autumn. We fill our eyes with the colors of scarlet, burnt orange and fire yellow. We fill our nostrils with the musky scent of fallen leaves. We know it will be many moons before springtime, when we can smell the earth once again.

[1997]

A best smell: boat motor fuel and lake water.

Inland Hurricane

The sun shines now, and hardly a fallen leaf stirs. It's hard to believe that, the day before yesterday, I was living in an inland hurricane.

It started with a gloomy drizzle. The wind blew and blew. Yet by 9:00 a.m., the air dried up and the sun glinted through magnificent grey clouds racing low across the skies.

Walking weather. I bundled up, but when I reached the top of our moraine, I shed my coat and hat. It had reached sixty degrees or so, and I was in the center of the loudest noise I've ever heard.

I stood in the woods and listened to the trees talk. They roared. I could hear no other sound – no truck beeps from the quarry beyond, no car noises from the highway, no industrial sounds from the hospital across the road. For once in my life, all I could hear was the sound of nature.

It was wonderful.

By 4:30 that day, our home was without electricity, and I was again struck with awe for nature, but in a different way. My house became a strange place: not a modern dwelling full of conveniences but a large, dark cave that grew gradually colder. My daughter and I groped about with flashlights and my grandmother's oil lamp. ("It was my grandma's job, when she was a little girl, to wash the chimney," I told Anna.)

The minute I knew I couldn't have it, I wanted hot soup for supper. I was in for an evening of quietness and cold toilet seat experiences. I had been washing clothes and wound up hanging two loads of wet laundry on the lines in the basement. I put a blanket around the cage holding our four baby chickens down there, hoping they'd survive.

Good thing we're campers. That night, Mike and I put on soft caps and sweats and huddled under our feather comforter. We invited Anna to join us, but she chose to snuggle with the dog under her own comforter.

I thought about Grandma Hoerig, growing up in Theresa, Wisconsin without electricity. I thought about the Indians who lived on my land when my "Grandfather" oak was a sapling back in the 1700s. I had a *tiny* feeling for what their lives must have been like.

We awoke the next morning to a cold house. Anna and Mike went to the YMCA to shower. I planned to buy dry ice for the freezer and gallons of water to flush the toilet before I left for work.

But at 7:30 the electricity came on and the sun began to blaze. Rescued. Thank God.

[1998]

A best smell: rain air.

Autumn

Two enormous spider webs are woven in the corners of the big double doorway leading into my barn. When I go at night to close in the chickens, I shine my flashlight on the webs. I catch two giant fat spiders working, working. I know it is autumn.

Squirrels scamper on grass, up trees, across roads, everywhere, with little mouths stretched around big acorns. I know it is autumn.

The cricket cacophony reaches a raucous crescendo. Whole fields of soy turn gold overnight. I know it is autumn.

It finally rains, and trees begin to give up their green. In the quarry lake I see a Monet reflection of color, color, color. I know it is autumn.

The humidity of August is gone, and I can breathe again. I go out for a night walk, where even in the dark there is no mistaking this for a spring evening. The night smells of musky fallen leaves. I know it is autumn.

A deer is hit by a car on the highway right in front of me. It is time for rutting, time for bow hunters. It's time for deer to run – because it is autumn.

Birds gather like black snow covering my yard. They fill in my elm tree with chatter. They are flocking – because it is autumn.

I hear the whish whish of wings overhead and even without looking up, I know they belong to Canada geese flying south because it is autumn.

The grass finally stops growing and I can forget about mowing. My dog sheds her summer coat and I mow the house of her white fluffy fur that appears like grass everywhere – because it is autumn.

For a few last weeks, I hang laundry on the line outside. For a precious little while, I drink the scent of bed sheets dried in sun and breeze. Intoxicating. Yet this will end because it is autumn.

My husband and I hurry our weekends fixing, shoring up, patching, protecting our home against winter's long battering. We finally end our putting-off because it is autumn.

In a few months, a white blanket will cover our mistakes and our accomplishments as householders. So we cherish this precious time, this beautiful season, this autumn.

[1998]

Liam and Oliver flinging leaves, 2013

A best smell: fresh-cut grass.

Deer Hunting

I hunt for deer all year 'round. I don't shoot them, but I like to look at them.

I have searched for the "V" shape of their heads facing me from a half-mile across the marsh in Menomonee Park. I have strained to hear antlers clicking against each other during rutting season. I have waited and watched for a second deer after one has bounded across the road. And I have smiled at their white tails like flags bouncing away.

I track the deer on my land. I watch how their hoof marks change with floods and droughts, with snows and melts. I see how my dog's prints change as they become days old, and thus I learn the look of older and newer tracks.

I find bare branches in the woods, where bucks have rubbed the velvet from their antlers. I search the brush for shed antlers, with no luck so far. The smaller woodland animals beat me to the prize, pouncing quickly on the antlers and their rich food stores.

Everything changes in October when the leaves drop. The sun shines brighter and harsher through empty limbs. I can spy into a secret world in the woods that was hidden from me all summer.

In November, when I see a deer, everything is slow and subtle. The deer moves slightly. I see only a change in the quality of brown.

Usually I hunt the deer, but once in a rare while they come to me. At dusk a month ago, a huge buck came lumbering into my back yard as if it were his bedroom. He ambled right into the stand of tall grasses between my yard and my neighbor's. Then he disappeared.

I quietly left my house and walked toward him, along the grasses. No movement. I sang. No movement.

Finally I walked around in back of him. There he nestled, between two big thistle plants, ready for a nice night's nap. I counted at least ten points on those antlers.

I stared. He stared.

"Boy, are you beautiful," I finally said.

That was enough for him. He ran and leaped away, passing right next to our tool shed and leaping as high as its roof – at least six feet. That's my ten-point buck story.

[1998]

Everyone from Wisconsin knows that when you're out of cheese, it's time to go to the grocery store.

Fruit Flies

There was a time I felt embarrassed by fruit flies in my kitchen. Dawn St. George changed that. She was dating a friend of the family, and the first time he brought her to visit, my husband and I had been doing a lot of canning. Fruit flies were everywhere, infuriating me, floating about in that lazy way of theirs that seems so aimless but must be full of fruit-fly-purpose. Anyone who has ever tried to get rid of fruit flies knows it's impossible. They're too small for fly swatters; you have to wait for frost or famine.

I could see that Dawn noticed them right away. Inwardly I shrank. Then her face brightened and she said, "Fruit flies! They take me back to my childhood. We lived on a farm right where Mayfair mall stands now. The kitchen is always full of fruit flies on a farm in September."

The way Dawn went on about them, fruit flies were a sign of a good and healthy home. After inwardly shrinking, my chest began to swell.

At the height of our canning era, Mike and I put up three hundred jars of pickles, tomatoes, applesauce, and I can't remember what-all-else. We took pictures of each other posing beside the colorful quarts and pints that were lined up like soldiers on the counter top and kitchen table. As if defeated by the produce, I posed lying down and Mike posed holding one of his aching feet.

It was the 1980s, our children were small, Mike's garden was big, and we were twenty years younger.

Since then, the garden has disappeared, we've bought a glass-top stove that we discovered makes it impossible to use a canning kettle, and our children have grown. I can't figure out why we're more busy instead of less, but it's true.

Then last summer we joined the Springdale Farm community-supported agriculture project in Plymouth, Wisconsin. Every week from May into December, we get a half-share of produce from the farm.

Once again, my counters are full of colorful organic stuff that makes my mouth water. I've experimented with vegetables I never heard of before. Once again it's a race between the fruit flies and me. Sometimes I fall behind and we have to do serious vegetable rescue.

But it's a good and healthy kitchen. Dawn would love it.

[2003]

Once I took back roads from Markesan to Wisconsin Dells. It was so beautiful off the expressway – I thought I was in Ireland!

There is a Way to Get Through November

November in Wisconsin is bleak. Leaden sky. Cold air. Whipping wind. Icy rain. We grumble. This transition from autumn to winter is hard on us. Once we're settled into full winter, we gain courage. We become strong. We deal with cumbersome layers of clothing, cold car seats, and the job of chipping ice off windshields.

November is the locking: transition time, neither fall nor winter. Mother Nature needs time to lock up for her long sleep to come.

There's a trick to getting through this grim time. It lies in focusing on *sound*. A wonderful sound is approaching, and it exists only in the *cold*. It is our privilege to hear it.

Think about it.

For every season, there is a sound. In March, the night awakes with the chirping of spring peepers – tiny frogs living in a wetland near you. This is my favorite sound in the world. Intoxicating.

Around that time, the morning air is so raucous with bird calls that I need ear plugs to sleep past 4:00 a.m.

In July and August, if you are lucky enough to be near a marsh, the night explodes with the lusty calls of bullfrogs and their mates.

Eventually the frogs calm down and crickets take over: a symphony of chirruping, in different tones and tempos.

If August is hot enough, and it always is where I live, a racket of cicadas fairly splits open the humidity rising from the earth. Their noise is an extended siren.

In September, if you close your eyes, you'll hear two things falling to the earth: apples and acorns. You might even detect a horse chestnut coming in for a landing.

In October and November, the most gentle sound of all brushes your ears: leaves falling, falling, falling.

Then from December through February comes the most beautiful sound of all: the sound of silence. The stillness almost hurts your ears on a night right after a snowfall. Moonlight illuminates the white on the ground, on trees and shrubs and houses. You can take a silent walk in the middle of the night, and you don't need a flashlight.

It takes some doing, but we can talk ourselves into looking forward to winter. November is the doorway.

[2012]

In all the old things I have, I see stories. I look at the oil lamp on my piano and remember my Grandma Hoerig telling me how she cleaned that lamp every week – and how exciting it was when electricity came down the road toward her family farm in Theresa.

When March Comes in Like a Lion...

Worst March ever. I hereby solemnly swear that I will never again complain about:

Flower beds that need weeding.
Singing birds waking me up at 4:00 a.m.
Hot blacktop burning my bare feet.
Hot sand burning my bare feet.
Barefoot encounters with thistles.
Barefoot encounters with gravel.
Balmy winds overturning a lamp.
Tornado warnings.
Being stung by a fat wasp while I pick tomatoes.
Too many tomatoes to can.
Too many loads of clothes to fit on the outside wash line....

Too many zucchini foundlings left on my doorstep.
My hens laying too many eggs.
Ants sharing a picnic lunch.
My daughter getting too heavy for her seat on the back of my bike.
Getting poison ivy walking through the woods.
Lying in bed at night with no sheets over me, trying not to move because it's so sticky-hot.
Slugs.
Spiders.
Shutting the drapes to the sun and sitting directly in front of an electric fan, my hair soaking wet from my second shower of the day....

Dusty window screens.
Barn smells.
Crickets chirping in chorus all night.
The fact that the grass has gone to seed again.

The fact that the back yard is soggy again (We should only grow a tamarack tree).

The fact that the house needs re-staining.

The fact that the barn and house eaves are full of hornet nests.

Sunburn.

My car becoming a sauna.

Steering wheel hand-burn ....

There are two items I must exclude from this list. I cannot promise not to moan about mosquito bites, or about subzero freezer sections in violently air-conditioned grocery stores.

As for the rest of what we loosely term "summer" in these parts, well, I'm ready for it to be so hot out that the rain feels warm.

This little writing is merely a pledge to myself that I won't bellyache next summer when we're talking dew point instead of wind-chill.

[1989]

Ralph Bronner lived in Menomonee Falls and was the eccentric son of the more-eccentric Emmanuel Bronner, who founded Dr. Bronner's Soaps. Ralph often spoke to college groups and always said the same thing: "Stay HUMAN!"

The True Hardy-Lifers

Once again Mike's Prediction has held true. Some folks may have their doubts, but it's been our experience that you can set your calendar by Mike's Prediction.

You see, according to my husband, we have only two weeks of below-zero weather in Southeast Wisconsin. Around these parts, that weather rolled in around January 2 and out around the 16th. So any nay-sayers must admit that for this year at least, Mike had a pretty accurate prediction.

Living in below-zero weather is something we Wisconsinites tolerate but never quite get used to. We need to know there's an end in sight.

But I've lived other places – Norfolk, Virginia, and Rome, Italy – where people would laugh if they heard that you could tolerate even two days of below-zero weather, much less two *weeks*.

I saw snow in both places, and some bone-chilling damp weather, although never the teeth-freezing bitterness we know in Wisconsin. And when snow comes to places like Virginia and Italy, we Wisconsinites have to laugh.

There they are, those Italian or Virginian hardy-lifers, out in their après-ski boots and garden hoes, trying to clear their walks. There are no snow plows, so a three-inch snowfall can mean school is closed for days. It's best to stay off the roads, because what warm-weather motorists don't know is that *you must learn to drive all over again each winter!* They drive way too fast and way too close. They build snowmen immediately because they're so excited about the snowfall. Here in Wisconsin, if our family hasn't built a snowman by February, we figure we'll still get a chance in March.

It must be true what they say about warm weather thinning the blood, because after we had lived in Virginia for a year, our friend Mark Metscher came to visit. It was Thanksgiving, and we were freezing and wearing winter jackets. Mark couldn't believe we were cold. He walked around outside in shirtsleeves, exclaiming, "Sheesh, it's fifty degrees!"

There's something special about really, really cold weather. It's so dangerous that it's exciting. I realize again what a thin thread we hang from. If I were a survivalist, I don't think I'd live in Wisconsin.

Come summer, it's all a memory. Then it's time for Mike's Prediction about above-ninety-degree weather. You guessed it: two weeks.

[1999]

My dog, Maggie, with snow-covered nose, on our land, 2012.

"Bloom where you're planted" is a hard directive during the winter when you're planted in Wisconsin.

100

Go Outside, Beat the Blues
During Winter Doldrums

It was a little world, and it was all blue. I pressed my nose against glass to gaze at it, to become part of it, at least in my imagination. It was a small diorama at the old Milwaukee museum downtown, a classic marble building (now the Central Library) that had a totem pole out front. The diorama housed a village of tiny people at work and play, Eskimo people as I called them then. Their houses were made of snow, not of wood like the white Cape Cod I lived in. Their transportation was sled and dog, not a red 1953 Ford like our family used.

In the diorama, the people seemed to live in an atmosphere of blue, dark blue. Either the sun didn't shine at all that day, or the land simply took on a blue cast from so much snow and ice and so many clouds. I didn't care then about the explanation. It was my favorite place in the museum.

During the month of December 2000, I felt like I was living in that little diorama. It snowed almost every day. When it snowed, it usually snowed all day long. I've never seen a succession of days where such light, fluffy snow fell. There were no driving blizzards, no wet, heavy flakes.

Nearly every weekday morning before work during the past year and a half, my husband and I have spent about forty-five minutes outside. In summer we go biking, in spring and fall we walk, and in winter we go snowshoeing.

I've discovered that my antidepressant is my time outdoors. The hardest part is getting out of bed; when we bundle up, we're not cold (at least not after the first five minutes). The trick is to keep our coats, hats and scarves on a hook so we can put them on with our eyes half-closed.

It's like we're living in that blue diorama now, especially at 5:30 a.m. when we begin our trek. Sometimes I think about those Inuit people who live in that dark blue land. As we snowshoe along before dawn, it's incredibly mysterious and beautiful.

Sometimes, as I'm tugging my snowshoe out of deep powder, I wonder to myself, "What am I *doing*?" Then I look out at the tree silhouettes on the snowy landscape. Or I look at my husband's sweet form in that snowmobile suit, with the earflap hat on top.

And I know that the blue world is okay. I can do this, at least for a time.

[2001]

We moved from Wisconsin to Virginia for the weather. We threw away our snow shovels. It took us three years to figure out that family trumps weather. We moved back home to Wisconsin. And got new snow shovels.

Starting the Day on the Fox

I like starting my day in a different head.

Today, February 5, my husband and I walked on the frozen Fox River, right along the Bugline trail. It's been such a snowless, mild winter that this was only the second time Mike wore his boots and snowmobile suit. His moon-explorer outfit slowed him down as we walked from our house, across the neighbors' front yards, to the river.

Once on the ice, he sped up – or maybe I slowed down due to my fear of slipping and falling.

I had walked the Fox alone last Friday as snow fell on my head – a beautiful experience – but I kept stepping through the top layer of ice, down to the second layer about four inches below. It was jarring. I kept grunting "*Uh!*" every time I popped through. I pulled the muscles in my left calf when my right foot sank.

Today, however, the ice was thicker. We broke through only once. And a snow covering, maybe two inches, kept us from slipping. The river is such a different path from the route that is our usual path – the Bugline trail, an old railroad right of way.

The Bugline is straight while the river meanders. So we meandered.

The Bugline is wide, but at some points the river is only about a yard across, so Mike and I took turns walking in front.

The Bugline is public (although we don't meet many folks before dawn, at five degrees Fahrenheit). The river is private, so I had the hope of meeting some deer, a flock of turkeys, a great horned owl, a rabbit or vole.

A man-made split rail fence runs along the Bugline. The river's border is made of puffy snowbanks and extravagantly abundant buff-colored grasses. The blades of the grasses are thick and soft: a cushy bed.

We walked in silence. Sometimes I hummed a hymn, my theme song for when I'm outside: "...for Love is lord of heaven and earth. How can I keep from singing?" But today the song wasn't in my head. Instead, the Indians were there. I wondered about how they survived along this river in winter when the giant oaks near us were saplings.

"Can you imagine," I asked Mike, "getting up hungry and having to invent a bow and arrow? Can you imagine how hard it must have been to fashion something strong enough to bring down a big animal?"

We talked about sinew and about sharpening arrow points. When the thought of sinew started grossing me out, I switched my focus to animal tracks.

We tracked a trail of a dog-like animal whose paw prints were much bigger than our dog's – a large coyote, maybe. Or a wolf? There were highways created by the small feet of mice and voles and rabbits. It seems all animals are creatures of habit, following the same routes again and again. Deer tracks were everywhere, even on the frozen river. Some of the tracks were very fresh, but we spied no deer.

We eventually got tired of scrambling over deadfalls on the river, so we clambered up to the Bugline, then along a path through corn fields and fence rows, and at last to the top of the moraine toward our land. The flock of turkeys had left their giant tracks in the fence line and in the cornfield itself. Usually the turkeys are more secretive; for them to emerge from hiding, their pickings must be getting slimmer and slimmer.

The great horned owl we sometimes see was done hunting and gone by the time we got to his tree.

The sun emerged, blazing orange, and the sky was painted in wild pinks and blues.

Finally, on our own land, we saw one shy deer, running, his white flag up. By the time we stomped off our boots in the screen porch, we had spent one hour walking outside, never once treading road or sidewalk.

How different was our morning adventure compared to the rest of the day we'd spend in the tame indoors.

I like starting my day in a different head.

[2002]

The hardest thing I've ever taught myself, and the most essential as a Wisconsin resident, is to love winter.

Hard Winter

We thought
it was such an easy winter
until we found
lying in a snowy thicket
the head of a young buck,
partially devoured,
nubs of antlers
covered by rough fur.

[2006]

*"I don't want to dance with any woman who doesn't
know the meaning of the word 'galoshes,'" said Pete, a
grey-haired man in my tango class. We were laughing
together about old guys pursuing young women.*

The Difference Between
Cold and *Really* Cold

Doe at our backyard feeder – in daytime! - 2013

When you live in Wisconsin, you understand the difference between cold and really cold. Cold is when you wear gloves. Really cold is when you wear mittens so your fingers can keep cach other warm – or better yet, you wear mittens-over-gloves.

Cold is when you wear a hat and scarf. Really cold is when your teeth freeze no matter what you wear.

Cold is when it takes ten minutes for your car heater to warm up. Really cold is when your tires freeze flat on one side and go ka-chunk, ka-chunk as you limp along at ten miles per hour until they return to round.

Cold is when water freezes in the birdbath on your lawn. Really cold is when you see your breath in your home's front entry.

Cold is when the world turns white as snow blankets the trees. Really cold is when the world turns to glass as ice coats the trees.

Cold is when there's no sound outdoors. Really cold is when the wind howls.

Cold is when snow wafts to the ground. Really cold is when snow goes sideways.

Cold is when the outdoor thermometer reads thirty degrees. Really cold is when you can't read the thermometer because it's coated with icy snow.

Cold is when your morning walk outfit is long underwear, sweatpants, a turtleneck, a sweatshirt, a heavy coat, hat, scarf, mittens, socks and boots. Really cold is when you add snow pants and a second pair of socks to that outfit.

Cold is when the deer come to the feeder at dusk. Really cold is when they come in broad daylight.

Cold is when your snowshoes slide. Really cold is when they crunch.

Cold is when the sky is grey and you feel grey. Really cold is when the sky is sunny and you feel alive.

Cold is when you take a walk on a lake. Really cold is when you drive your truck on it.

Cold is when you gasp when the air hits your lungs. Really cold is when the air makes you cough.

Cold is when you come home from walking and the house feels warm. Really cold is when you come home from walking and the house feels hot.

Cold is when it's nice to build a fire in the fireplace. Really cold is when it's hard to start a fire because the wind is blowing down the chimney.

Cold is when it's a pain to go grocery shopping. Really cold is when you learn to invent from what's on hand.

[2013]

Part Four
Looking In and Out

The island – and its reflection - on Little Green Lake

Capture the Available Minute

All busy people are philosophers about time. I used to think I was the busiest person in the U.S. of A. But now that I know more people (and maybe now that I've grown up a bit), I've come to realize that most people in this country are busy – or at least they feel busy, which amounts to the same thing. I'm no longer busier than thou.

Jogging around the rim of a perpetually spinning top is rough on relationships. Because I believe that love is spelled T-I-M-E, I've become ferocious about guarding moments with my mate and with my children. The early deaths of my parents and younger brother seared a lesson onto my brain: "Life and time are our only true possessions."

The problem with feeling this way is that it takes me skipping right down the path of guilt. For years I've replied to my friends and to myself, as a rejoinder to "I don't have any time": "No one *has* any time; you have to *make* time."

I still believe that we create our own lives from the chunks we carve out of time. However, I used to lecture myself to a tune that went something like this: "You're not spending enough time with your children, Gail." Or: "You should talk more with Mike."

Should, should, should. Pressure and guilt. I felt burdened with nagging doubts about the time (love) I was giving.

Then last December I was privileged to hear a short talk in Brookfield given by Mary Linsmeier that freed me from that stifling guilt (well, most of it). Mary is the mother of eight, a marriage and family therapist, and founder of Linsmeier preschools in the Milwaukee area. I had invited her to speak to a group of single mothers with whom I work through HOPE Network. If we married mothers feel bad about being spread too thin, imagine how single mothers feel!

The question of "quality time" came up during Mary's presentation. She almost laughed.

"No one ever has enough time," she said. "Instead of feeling guilty about the quality hour that never happens, capture the available minute or two that you have with your child." She went on to explain how you can have a great heart-to-heart talk with your children while you do mundane kitchen chores together, for example.

Mary Linsmeier made me think in a new way about capturing the available minute.

I feel okay now if I get a bunch of phone calls in a morning; my preschool daughter and I color together while I attend to whatever telephone business is necessary. I've found that waiting rooms provide a great opportunity for me to read books to her. And although I love to read while I eat lunch (a bad "fat habit," according to experts), I've tried to make a practice of talking with Anna while we munch our peanut butter and jelly sandwiches.

A heck of a lot of "minute-capturing" goes on in the car. Mike and I have some of our best conversations as we drive places (usually the children are involved in their own talking, squabbling, or nonsense in the back seat). Many of our conversations are catch-up talk, where Mike and I bring each other up to date on what's happening in our lives. That isn't exactly gripping dialog, but it frees up our quiet time, after the kids are in bed, for the important stuff.

When I'm driving the boys here and there, I try to catch up with their lives too.

Maybe it's sacrilegious, but we've had at least two prayer meetings as a family in the car. I don't think God minds. You see, we have a tradition of prayer meetings each Sunday. But sometimes the day slips away. Then Sunday evening we're coming home from somewhere and it dawns on me that we've missed our meeting. I know it's not only a meeting with God but also a meeting with each other, and we need it. If by the time we get home it's going to be bedtime (or past bedtime), we have our prayer meeting right there. I tell a story from the Bible; we talk about our goals for the coming week and discuss how we did last week; we say prayers together. Thus sometimes our car is a cathedral.

Work projects are also a great time for minute-grabbing. My son Brian and I were painting the basement floor the other day, and I asked him to tell me all about the Charlie Chaplin film we had rented but which I didn't have a chance to see. My question got a conversation going, but my big togetherness plan backfired on me. Every time Brian talked, he stopped painting.

Whenever I feel that I have no time, I remind myself that we're all given twenty-four hours each day. And I try to catch those minutes as they fall.

[1988]

I'd rather have the love of a child than receive the Pulitzer Prize.

Pop was a Person

He told the worst jokes and the best jokes. He couldn't open a milk carton or an aspirin bottle. He was almost twice as old as I was when he died. Yet no barriers ever prevented us from talking, dancing, drinking, laughing together – two friends.

He taught me how to feel the tug of a fish on my line so we could fish in pre-dawn darkness on Big Muskego Lake in a wooden row boat we rented for a dollar. (We didn't use bobbers.)

He taught me how to build an igloo and how to dance a jitterbug.

He taught me respect for the English language – lay versus lie, me versus I.

He taught me positive thinking. When I went door to door selling Girl Scout cookies or candy bars for school, he taught me to ask people, "Do you want two or three?" instead of "Do you want any?" He assured me the worst thing they could say was "no."

He taught me the value of a dollar – "The money you spend today casts a shadow to the end of your life," he'd remind me.

He taught me self-determination – "Life is what you make it."

He taught me not to be phony and to recognize phoniness in people. "Be yourself," he'd say again and again. (Maybe that's why I was never a good actress.)

He chased away a lot of boyfriends (and I often breathed a sigh of relief). He made me angry, he made me proud.

He taught me to be honest – "The worst things you can do are to lie, cheat, and steal." He taught me never to compromise my values – "Do what's right because it's right; you need no other reason." And he taught me to speak up – "Stand up and be counted."

He taught me how a man should treat his wife and children – with love, respect, and humor.

He was my father and my teacher. I learned a lot from him because I knew his mind was open to learn from me. I think about my three children and hope I can be such a teacher and friend.

[1990]

Pop on Great Slave Lake, Northwest Territories, circa 1977

"A good worker rises to the top like cream rises to the top of a bottle of milk."   *– Ted Grenier, my dad*

Waking Up

Somehow it was hidden from me, my Irishness. It took me a long time to figure out why. I started putting the pieces together this summer, after a sixteen-year-old Irishman became part of my family.

In the years before my awakening, I was wearing blinders but didn't realize it. Like many American children, I enjoyed the fact that I had European roots. My father was raised in Taunton, Massachusetts, where Canadian French was spoken at home; my mother grew up in St. Michael's, Wisconsin, where German was spoken at home. Thanks to them, I learned a smattering of colorful expressions in German and French – spicier for me (even now) than their English equivalents.

Nearly every summer when I was growing up, we made the long car trip from our home in Milwaukee, Wisconsin, to Taunton, Massachusetts, to visit Pop's side of the family. We used the French Canadian names *Mémère* and *Pépère* for our grandmother and grandfather there.

Mémère spoke French with ease, and referred to herself as my "French grandmother." It's true that Mémère's mother's name was Marie Maurisset, very French. But her father was Thomas *McGrath*. As I grew older, I became interested in my ancestors and did a bit of research. However, I found genealogy a male-oriented journey that followed rivers of name-carriers and ignored smaller feminine streams along the way. Thus I learned about Greniers (my Pépère's side) but not about McGraths (my Mémère's side).

Mémère died a long time ago, and I have only a few stories I remember from her, sad stories. I don't recall her referring to being Irish, except maybe once to mention "cabbage hill" and to say that her family came to the U.S. during the potato famine, through Prince Edward Island in Canada.

Everything I remember from Mémère's lips is vague – stories about her infant siblings perishing from "summer complaint" after drinking milk that had been left on a sunny doorstep – her mother dying of a broken heart after losing yet another baby – Mémère living in foster homes and digging in garbage cans for food – going to school where nuns taught her perfect embroidery – and working on sweatshop sewing machines when she was older.

I think that for Mémère and probably for my dad, the word "Irish" meant "poor" or "looked down upon." I believe now that Mémère was *ashamed* to be Irish, so she tried to erase her Irishness. Pop, in turn, emphasized only his French roots to me. He once told me that his home town was divided between French and Irish; his parents' union was considered a mixed marriage. To blend in, Mémère became "French." I wish now that I had asked more about her Irishness.

Sometimes Mémère's voice became loud and bitter, she would drink and curse, and I stopped listening because it was too painful to be near her. I realize now that she left a legacy of sorrow. What she told me was sad enough; after she died, I learned that what she omitted was even sadder, beyond speaking.

Someone once explained this phenomenon to me as *generational sadness*. The immigrants came to America with boat loads of horror stories. Infant mortality was a fact of life; baby quilts weren't commonly made until well into the twentieth century. If parents had allowed themselves to *feel* the pain, they'd have gone crazy. So they taught themselves to push their emotions down, down, down.

But the feelings didn't go away. The sorrow was passed along namelessly, wordlessly to the next generation, and to the next. And with this mute grief came the "isms" we desperate humans use in our innocence and ignorance to bandage our wounds: alcoholism, materialism, fanaticism, on and on.

The year Mémère died, I happened to see a television documentary on Northern Ireland. The film showed young boys and girls who were growing up hard and hating in an environment of broken glass and rocks. Bombs and guns. I watched the images on the screen and felt as if my guts were being chewed. Suddenly, the nameless thing that had been hidden came to life for me. Part of me was Irish; the hurt and hatred on the screen was part of my story. The faces of those children figured into the generational sadness that Mémère bequeathed to me without speaking of it.

Last July, these feelings came to life in the form of a sixteen-year-old dark-haired, green-eyed student named Michael Uprichard, who traveled from Northern Ireland to live with my family. Michael and nineteen other Belfast-area teens were matched with Milwaukee-area host families for one month as part of the Ulster Project, a grassroots peacemaking effort.

Although we were new to it, the Ulster Project has been around for a while. In 1975, Reverend Kerry Waterstone founded it as an ecumenical peace program involving boys and girls fourteen to sixteen years old from Belfast's Roman Catholic and Protestant faith communities. I explain to my friends, "We bring 'em to Milwaukee, mix 'em up for a month, then send 'em back home." Follow-ups indicate the effort is working; Northern Irish teens who participate in the Ulster Project keep their inter-denominational friendships and avoid paramilitary groups when they return to Belfast.

At first I wanted our family to be part of the Project because it was part of peace-making. However, that motivation became less and less important as I got to know Michael more and more. I came to think of him as an uncorrupted young adult. He's a Protestant who was matched with our family because, although my

117

husband Mike and I were raised Catholic, we currently attend a Protestant church with our children.

Michael enjoys his cultural heritage, including traditional music and the Irish language – which are typically part of the Catholic learning experience in Northern Ireland. From the start of his visit, he talked intelligently and articulately about "the Troubles" he's lived with all his life. He compared Irish sectarian violence to U.S. gang fighting; I got a whole new perspective on a problem that has many explanations but no easy solution. He taught us about the I.R.A. (the Catholic Irish Republican Army) and the U.V.F. (the Loyalist/Protestant terrorists). We learned that "Catholic" and "Protestant" signify *political*, more than religious, divisions in Northern Ireland.

With his typical humor and fairness, Michael said things like, "I applied for a job at Pizza Hut but the I.R.A. blew it up; so they were only lookin' for people to scrape mozzarella off the road. Then the U.V.F. killed four people in five days because they were Catholic. The U.V.F. said it's because they were in the I.R.A. but that's a load of b.s."

Michael is easy-going, and he blended perfectly with our family (he called us "slightly mad" or "several pork pies short of a picnic"). As the hot days of July passed, we grew comfortable with one another, joking and poking good-natured fun. Michael and I had long talks that turned from bombs and politics to the simpler everyday things that make the world go 'round for ordinary people: weather, jobs, music, food, school, customs, families, accents, slang, philosophy, relationships, stars in the sky. I knew Michael had become one of my kids when I, all smiles, kicked him in the seat of his pants for a sassy remark he had made, all smiles too.

Michael played with our little Anna, hung out at a local restaurant with our older son Charlie; partied with our son Brian, who was Michael's teen host; went fishing with my husband Mike; and talked to our cats in his gentle Irish tones. What began as a "project" transformed into something more lasting and certainly more authentic: a *friendship*.

I was nearly lulled by all the fun and normalcy into forgetting what the Ulster Project was all about when, toward the end of July, someone in the Project told me about the Belfast tradition of kneecapping: shooting or drilling someone's knee if he refuses to join a paramilitary group. The victim often never walks again. Horrified, I asked Michael if he will be in danger of being kneecapped back home. He assured me that since he lives right outside Belfast, he shouldn't be threatened.

The day we sent Michael back to Belfast, we all drank "tearwater tea," to quote Arnold Lobel. I mean, we *drowned* in tears. The scene at the airport was worse than a funeral, a mess of red eyes, with wailing and weeping of teenage boys and girls, moms and dads, little brothers and sisters. We had to practically be torn apart when it was time for the plane to depart.

"I'll miss you so much," Michael said, hugging me.

I love you so much, I thought but couldn't say it. He knew, anyway. How close folks can grow in one short month. How easy to shed our walls when we know our time together is brief.

In the weeks since then, I've experienced a grieving I never anticipated and would have doubted had someone warned me. When Michael left, I lost a son and a friend. The pain of missing him was compounded by worry. I pushed the worry aside because I knew it wouldn't do any good. But still the pain got screaming bad. I became so depressed that down looked up to me. I knew I had to channel my grieving or I'd cease to be able to function.

So I turned to my Irish roots. I listened to Irish music. I went to the library and gobbled up everything I could find about Ireland – biographies and folklore and history. I drank another ocean of tearwater tea when I learned the *truth* about the potato famine: that the disaster that forced my Catholic ancestors to these shores was created not only by nature, as I had been taught, but by humans as well. The accounts I read about British treatment of the Irish were nearly as cruel as anything I've learned about the treatment of Native Americans by the Europeans who took over this continent.

At Milwaukee's Irish Fest the following August, I spent an hour arguing with an Irish Republican Army supporter, then another hour digging in the genealogy booth. I learned that McGrath is a name from the north of Ireland. Now I'm studying Irish Gaelic, and through this strange and beautiful language, unraveling some of the mysteries that were kept from me for so long. The language holds many clues into the Irish "personality." For example, "Good day" in Irish, translated, is "God be with you," and takes a response of "God and Mary be with you." The basis of Irish culture is *faith.*

In my Gaelic class I met a woman who, like me, has been on a journey of discovery through her Irish roots. She recommended a book called *Healing the Family Tree.* Inspired by the book, she and her father went to Irish sections of Boston and learned about the who and why of their family's hardships and shortcomings. Together they prayed for each family member and ancestor they came to "know." She told me that she witnessed a miracle: a dramatic change in her own father.

My life has been so full of miracles that I count on them. My friend Donna Eddy says that "coincidence" is God's middle name. It's no coincidence that I, a non-TV person, happened upon that documentary about Northern Ireland thirteen years ago – and found the images that began my awakening. It's no coincidence that I learned about the Ulster Project, a quiet endeavor with probably the least publicity in the world.

It's no coincidence that Michael blended in with my family in his gentle way, bringing a human dimension to all my wonderings about Ireland. And it's no coincidence that Michael is unburdened by prejudice, standing up for nonviolence at every turn. I know that even as I uncover harsh truths about Ireland past and present, Michael will be my "conscience" and keep me from hating. What good would it do for me to hate the British people who are the descendants of the oppressors of my ancestors? Little did I guess that the lessons of the Ulster Project would rub off on me!

Although I may never make the physical journey to Ireland, I'm sure I'll complete the pilgrimage into the past that I have begun. I'll do it for Mémère. I'll do it for me. I'll do it for all the confused grandchildren of famine survivors. I'll find words for Mémère's unspoken legacy of sorrow, so that the generational McGrath grief work may finally begin. Perhaps what I come to understand will help my family and me, so that we'll have less cause to drink and to curse.

Our summer Ulster Project mirrored life itself. Like the month-long Project, the time we *all* have with one another is short indeed. How close we can grow – and how much fun we can have – if we shed our walls.

I am Irish and American, Catholic and Protestant, oppressor and oppressed. How could I bear hatred for anyone? I could easily have been born into different circumstances.

My journey must be one of peace, for I believe in the saying, "If we search far enough into our family tree, we'll find only one root in all the world."

[1993]

The Painting Sandals

When I was young, Mum told me that painting made her body sore. I didn't understand what she meant.

I understand now.

Mum was my muse for painting and varnishing this week. I have her old painting sandals, all splotched with white and green and blue paint. I put them on and wore them a while, even though they aren't that comfortable. I wound up barefoot eventually, but I put Mum's sandals in the corner of the room while I worked.

She was there.

I know.

She's my guardian angel of painting.

Mike and I lived in Virginia as newlyweds. After three years there, we decided to move back to Wisconsin. It was a snap decision that we made one day while we were wallpapering. We were making a disaster of it and inventing new swear words. I got disgusted and said, "Mum would help us with this."

We moved back to Wisconsin that summer and had three years with Mum and Pop before they were killed in a car accident.

I'm glad they raised me to act on impulse.

[1994]

"Expect nothing, and you won't be disappointed."
– *Audrey Hoerig Grenier, my mother*

122

Hobo Life

We were sitting in the back yard, my son Brian and me, when I heard it. "Listen!" I said.

"Listen to what?" he asked.

"The train! Don't you hear it?"

The train tracks lie in the Town of Lisbon, far from our house. We hear the train whistles only on very still evenings when the wind and atmosphere are just right. "I love that sound," I told Brian.

"Why?" he asked. Brian is sixteen and knows that what his mom likes best is *quiet*, not noise. I had to think a moment. How could I explain why the sound of a distant train whistle moved me so?

I stammered: "Because – because it's the sound of freedom."

Of course Brian didn't understand. He hasn't lived the hobo life. If I could, I'd hop a freight train tomorrow, although it's not a safe proposition for a woman traveling alone in the U.S. But how I'd love to try the hobo life, if only for a while.

I spent almost a year of my life traveling on trains. I was nineteen and then twenty years old, a college junior studying in Rome, Italy – my first time away from home. The university staff encouraged us to travel, saying it was part of our education. We were young, we traveled light, we traveled cheap. We stayed at dollar-and-a-half-a-night *pensiones*. We traveled second class on trains. Sometimes the trains were crowded with soldiers or local people on holiday, and we couldn't find a seat, so we stood. It was fine.

The sound of the train was the best part: ka-chunk, ka-chunk, monotonous, lulling us to sleep. During one long journey, I climbed into the luggage carrier to lie down. The luggage carrier was a net suspended above the train seat in an enclosed compartment where two seats faced one another. It made a good hammock, and the ka-chunk of the train made a great lullaby. The best sleeps are train sleeps.

I wasn't a real hobo. I paid for my rides. I had a roof to return to when my travels were done. I didn't cook my meals campfire-style by the side of the tracks. I didn't write in hobo-code on the sides of boxcars. But I got a taste of freedom. Those college people were right: traveling is part of an education. It probably doesn't matter where or how you eat miles. When you wander, you learn about yourself. You learn to travel light. You communicate in the universal human language of courtesy: a smile and a thank you. You learn about affluence and poverty and you get a perspective on your own lot in life. You experience travel-weariness and travel-grit. I traveled so much when I was twenty that I lost my wanderlust. Only recently, now that my children are older, have I tasted it once again.

Not long ago, I had to stop for a train at the crossing in the Town of Lisbon. I sat, car engine idling, while I absently watched the hoppers, gondolas, boxcars, and flatcars waddle by. Suddenly my eyes unblurred. Passing right in front of me was an open boxcar. Sitting in the door opening, swinging his legs, sat a young dark-haired man. He looked like Jack Kerouac and he gazed ahead at the track winding beyond.

It was the first time I'd seen someone who was hitching a ride in a boxcar. I was amazed that some folks still answer the call of the train whistle. I hear the call but I don't answer. Seems to me, though, that even those who stay put may gaze ahead at the track winding beyond.

[1994]

A best sound: train whistle in the distance.

Humbled by Nature

Thunder growled across the dark land. Far in the distance, flashes of lightning lit up the whole sky. It was warm. Rain fell only a drop here, a drop there. It would be a while before the storm hit, plenty of time to walk my dog. So Maggie and I set out, into the night.

A thick forest lies beyond the few homes of my neighbors on Custer Lane in Menomonee Falls. Once I passed the last house, I was in a tunnel of trees. My husband and I call this Murkwood, apologies to J.R.R. Tolkien. The only light I saw was dim, a quarter mile down the road, where Murkwood opens up onto the highway.

I threw my face to the sky. I felt like a kid again. Like most women, I love the powerful feeling of wind in my hair, the balmy breeze of a humid summer night, the time right before a storm. I plug into the electricity in the air. Yet, when the rare car comes roaring along, I feel like a deer in headlights. I want to run.

This particular night, I didn't have that feeling. Everything was perfect. Even Maggie, leashless, walked beside me like a dog trained to heel, which she isn't. We strolled along my road toward its end at Highway 74.

It was into this perfect night that I saw the doe walk onto the highway. My only thought was of her beauty, a lovely picture for the driver of the oncoming car. But the car didn't slow down.

I watched, not believing, as the vehicle hit the doe with an awful "pop," and kept going. Still alive, the deer couldn't drag herself off the road. She was big. She lay across almost the entire lane of traffic. By then, I was close enough to signal a few cars away with my flashlight.

As cars gathered and police were called, the doe looked at us humans with calm eyes. She made no sound. I waited in the warm rain, now pouring, until the officer arrived. Then I left.

Later as Maggie and I walked back through Murkwood, I heard the shot. It was louder than the thunder.

The doe lives in my mind. I keep trying to find a lesson other than the obvious ones about deer overpopulation, driving safety, and the necessity of predators in orange.

I keep seeing her eyes. Maybe my lesson lies in her calm. May I meet suffering with such acceptance.

[1998]

I'm always happy when I wake up and I'm above ground.

The Dance of Life

What do you do when you escape the Grim Reaper? You dance.

I saw that truth this summer in my own family, and again when a Holocaust survivor spoke at my daughter's school.

First the family story. It was last June and we were invited to a family wedding in Milwaukee. About a month before that, my husband, Mike, had gone through quadruple bypass heart surgery – at the age of forty-eight. At the wedding, he still looked a little green.

But the day was beautiful and the night held promise – a live band was going to play. A live band instead of a disc jockey, playing songs we've heard a thousand times. Mike and I love to dance, but we hadn't danced in so long ....

We started out slowly. A little dance here, a little dance there. Finally we got going, and we were still dancing strong at midnight when Mike's joy translated itself into the craziest dance I've ever seen. He held his arms straight at his sides, with feet together, knees stiff, and he *boinged* up and down all over the place, grinning like – like – a boinging dancer.

Mike's dance shouted, *"I'm alive!"*

At my daughter's school I encountered another man who feels that way: Jay Sommer. He was the speaker I heard there, a Holocaust survivor who recently published the tale of his experiences in a book called *The Journey to the Golden Door.*

Jay is full of humor, full of joy. He said, "We should remember the Holocaust, but we should also remember people who were kind. At a time when things were very dark, they brought some light."

Jay said that those who survived places like Auschwitz met at certain gathering points after their liberation. There he found his brother. It was a time of enormous joy but also sadness, for he learned then that another brother had been killed.

Jay's surviving brother informed him that his girlfriend had also survived and there would be a friend's wedding in a few days.

Jay explained, "This meant a new start for us. We decided we would have no sad stories at the wedding. We danced so hard that the floor was moving up and down – and it was a cement floor."

"*We're alive!*" was the dance they danced.

[1998]

Every child is born knowing how to dance.

Dancing in the Door

This past weekend was my first experience of the Door County Folk Festival, although it's been around now for twenty years. I found out I've really been missing something.

My husband, Mike, and I folk danced regularly for the first twenty years of our marriage, and we got our kids involved. But for the last seven years, we've been mostly danceless.

Then about a month ago, I got a brochure in the mail, sent by an old folk dancing friend, Wendy Seaman. The brochure advertised the folk festival, and I thought, *Why not?*

Mike and our two local kids, Charlie and Anna, agreed to come, although Anna hardly remembered that she folk danced when she was a little girl. She's fifteen now, and we stopped dancing half her lifetime ago. Charlie, who is twenty-three, remembers it well; he used to perform with his dad in a little multi-ethnic dance troupe.

We hooked up the pop-up camper and off we went, for adventures unknown. Typical of our family's style, we underestimated the amount of time it would take to get to Door County. Plus, we had a cat escape at the last minute and had to do reconnaissance.

So we slid into our first workshop fifteen minutes late, still hauling the camper and not even checked into our campground. Poor Mike had to find a spot to park car and camper on the beautiful but tourist-filled Ephraim streets.

It was all uphill from there. Besides the traditional international folk dancing we did on Friday, all four of us participated in a Lindy hop workshop Friday and a Lindy dance party Friday evening. On Saturday, Anna and I did Middle East movement (translated: belly dancing). All I can say is *wow*!

Anna was underwhelmed, to say the least, by the mostly Balkan/Bulgarian dancing we encountered.

But she loved the belly dancing, and the ethnic dance party Saturday night won her over. It was a thrill to see her transformation. Her feet moved perfectly with the music, and she smiled the whole time she danced.

Charlie too was ecstatic. "It brought it all back for me," he said with a smile.

He dragged me to a Balkan singing workshop, something I never would have tried on my own. My neck and arms tingled as I became one of a large chorus in five-part harmony. I found myself *belting*.

Our workshop leaders explained that the loud Balkan style evolved from women shouting the songs as they worked in the fields. They had to project their voices – almost like bleating sheep – in order to hear each other. They sang out the dramas of their lives, all their loves and struggles. It was really fun to holler-sing the Bulgarian words and hear our voices echo off the high ceiling – probably more fun than working in a field, I'm guessing.

All of us humans started as tribal people dancing around campfires and singing in work fields. Our bones remember. I don't know the names of all the traditional instruments, but when I hear them, I feel my blood singing.

Opa!

[1999]

If a non-dancer marries a dancer, that's a mixed marriage.

The Large Trousers

It was depressing to pack my trousers. I held them up before folding them, my arms extended, garment at nose height. A giant, square pants-ass stared me in the face. And I had tried, really tried, to lose weight for this trip to the Land of the Beautiful.

A Menomonee Falls Patio Players costume seamstress once told me the average size for Wisconsin women is 14. I fit right in.

Dang. I folded the pants and plunked them into my suitcase. How was I going to not stick out like a Cheesehead in Los Angeles? How could a Menomonee Fallsian blend into Hollywood? And later, how could I hide my girth at the home of my thin brother and his thin wife in Escondido?

Ah, no use in self-flagellation. I packed some unobtrusive clothing, shut the suitcase, sucked in my stomach, and planned to keep sucking in for the next five days.

The direct flight was so quick that I had ants in my pants only for the last hour.

After Mike and I landed in LAX, we experienced culture shock even before we walked to Baggage. Here and there throughout the airport were women who looked like they had all visited the same plastic surgeon. They looked nearly identical, with dyed blonde hair, very skinny bodies, knee-high spike-heeled boots or mukluk-like "Uggs" (even thought it was seventy five degrees outside), and very made-up faces with pouty lips and cats' eyes. I'm not exaggerating when I say their faces were scary-looking, like Halloween masks.

I had to visit the necessary room. In the stall next to me was a woman obviously vomiting. I was immediately afflicted with Midwest concern for others.

When I emerged from my stall, I started to say, "Are you okay? Do you need help?" – when her stall door opened and out emerged one of the skinniest of the pouty-lipped creatures I had just seen outside.

I shut up. I understood immediately: she had been purging. Puking her meals was the secret to her stick-thin jeans! Bulimia.

I thought about the large trousers waiting for me in my suitcase back in Baggage. I realized I loved those pants.

[2006]

One of my health goals: never be more than one axe handle wide.

Fighting Bad Guys with a Smile

A mugger almost got me one time
outside Northridge mall in Milwaukee –

Me – middle-aged, small, white, female,
arms laden with heavy bags –
Christmas gifts.

The mugger – young, big, black, male,
someone I'm "supposed" to fear.

Before I saw him,
I *felt* him
behind me.
Somehow I knew he had walked
fast, diagonally across the parking lot
to catch up with me.

I did
what came naturally,
what I'd do without thought
to anyone who had hurried
to meet me:

I turned.
My eyes met his eyes.
I smiled.
I said "Hi!"
as if he were a friend
I hadn't seen in a long time.

His face held no expression.
He zipped his eyes away and
zipped his body away
diagonally across the parking lot

back the way he had come.

Last night my daughter Anna called
to tell me her friend and co-worker was dead –
twenty-one years old, delivering
Jimmy Johns sandwiches
at night in Milwaukee,
shot twice in the chest,
robbed.

The cops found
a young dead body,
no wallet, no I.D.,
a Jimmy Johns car nearby.

They called Jimmy Johns
and asked "Are you missing a driver?"

Anna said several other drivers
had been robbed lately –
they carry all their money to the end
of their shifts.

Someone knew.

Did Anna's friend resist
when the bad guys hurried up to rob him?
Would a smile and a dumb "Hi!" have saved his life?
We'll never know.

Now there are two parents
like Mike and me
mourning their young son,
the same age as our Anna.

I ache for the hole in their hearts

and I wish

all the bad guys could be
disarmed with a smile.

I wish
all the good guys
all the poor college kids trying to make a buck
delivering sandwiches
could protect themselves
with a smile on their faces
instead of
a gun in their pockets.

[2006]

Freedom: not having to lock your car or house – still happens in some places in Wisconsin.

September 11 Blood Drive
May Define a Generation

That Tuesday was the kind of perfect day for which September is famous: clear air, no humidity, blue sky, sunshine. The biggest news on the radio was Michael Jordan's return to basketball. I hung four loads of wash to dry. I was content.

My husband's telephone call changed all that. He told me the news. He said I should turn on the television. I didn't want to watch. I didn't watch the news during all of the Vietnam War; why should I look now? What good would it do?

I cried. I prayed. And finally I turned on the TV, unable to resist watching the horrific images again and again and again. I canceled my writing class at Waukesha County Technical College.

The news people said hospitals in New York were out of blood. I called the Blood Center and got a recording.

I went to pick up my daughter, Anna, from her high school, Pius XI, in Milwaukee. She had spent the morning watching TV, talking, and praying with teachers and students there. She was glad to leave. We drove to the Blood Center in downtown Milwaukee, one among many cars streaming in.

A man greeted us in the parking lot. "We've had a bomb threat," he told us. "Try our center on Watertown Plank Road."

At that center, we found a parking lot packed with cars and a waiting room full of people sitting on the floor, the chairs, the tables. They were watching the news and talking. One young man said, "Can you imagine how many families, how many children, this involves?"

The center wouldn't take our blood. I had donated too recently, and Anna was too young.

Anna and I talked, the two of us, as we drove home. The streets seemed surreal with their ordinariness. It was hard to drive, hard to focus. We passed an auto accident, probably caused by someone who couldn't concentrate.

I'm glad my daughter is almost seventeen. I would not want to have to live through this with a younger child. I think that Tuesday was the last day of Anna's childhood. The attack on America will certainly be the defining moment for her generation, as Kennedy's assassination was for mine. Things will never be the same for her and her friends. It's hard to imagine that they'll become more jaded than they are now, but I'm afraid that's inevitable.

However, the Blood Center was full of young people. I think they understand that things are different now. I think they have a sense of history. Anna and I both felt better for having seen them there.

When we got home, Anna lay on her bed. I lay next to her and hugged her, rubbed her back. I thought about all the mothers that can't hug their daughters now.

During the Vietnam War, we expressed our grief with black arm bands. Villagers abroad still wear them when a loved one has died. It's a time for black arm bands once again.

But it's also a time of hope, because of what America really is. America is those young people that I saw at the Blood Center.

[2011]

There aren't many opportunities to give an hour and save three lives. Donating blood is the easiest volunteer work I know of.

Be Here Now

I was at a party and met a young man who's a student at Marquette University. I told him I went there too, long ago. He seemed interested; we had a nice connection. Then suddenly he looked down at his iPhone.

He was lost to me. I didn't exist.

I've had it.

It's not only young people. Older folks do it too: suddenly shift attention from their surroundings in order to stare at a machine in their hand. I feel jumpy with all the multi-tasking going on around me.

And I feel insignificant.

If I'm boring people, I'd like them to think of a clever way to extricate themselves from my presence, as I must do when I'm tired of a conversation. Why shouldn't they suffer like I do?

My friend Karen Cluppert tells me to lighten up. She says, "They don't even realize they're doing it."

Well, someone needs to tell them: *This is rude! Look into people's eyes! Be a human being! Be here now!*

At the party with the Marquette student, I bit my tongue. I never have the courage to say anything; I'm always in shock when someone suddenly looks away from me and switches focus to an electronic gadget.

Soon after the party, I happened to rent the movie "Shaun of the Dead." It was one of the funniest films I've ever seen, full of laughs and terrific movie zombies.

After I watched that movie, I made a connection: people who suddenly gaze down at machines in their hands look like *zombies*. They lose the human connection to those around them. It's like they're possessed by a power greater than themselves. They stiffen. They stare. They become passive and helpless, like the Eloi when the Morlocks run the siren in "The Time Machine."

iPhone zombies don't moan like movie zombies, but I'm ready to. I can't take it anymore.

So I've come up with an assortment of quick comments I might fling – if I gather the courage – the next time I'm talking to an iPhone zombie who enters an altered state:

1. "Sorry – I didn't mean to keep you from your machine."

2. "Am I boring you?"

3. (No comment at all; turn on my heel and walk away, or leave the table.)

4. (While hovering my hand and wristwatch over the face of the iPhone) "Do you need the time? It's 5:15."

5. "Is Mommy calling?"

6. "Helloo-oo! Remember me?"

7. "Remember when we used to go minutes without one?"

8. "Did the Morlocks ring the siren?"

9. "BE HERE NOW."

I actually tried comment #9 one time. I was with someone who pulled out her phone and started fiddling with it. I caught her eye and said, "Be here now."

She didn't know what I was talking about.

I was a senior in college when the book *Be Here Now* came out. Someone handed it to me and said, "Pass this book on when you finish it. Sign your name inside the cover and ask the next reader to do the same."

I had never seen a book like it. It was big and fat, with a purple cover featuring a mandala and the words "Remember" and "Be Here Now." The brown crinkly book pages reminded me of paper grocery bags. On those crinkly pages were words in all kinds of typefaces and sizes, plus illustrations.

I read a lot of the tome, but I never digested every word. It didn't take long to get the principle of the thing: *be here now*.

I passed the volume along, but I never forgot it. Maybe twenty years later, I purchased *Be Here Now* and gave it to a friend who needed to find a way to slow down. I don't think the book has ever been out of print. It was written by Richard Alpert, who changed his name to Ram Dass. For Ram Dass, the writing was a religious manifesto of sorts.

For me, it was simply a recipe for happiness. Be here now. I've tried my whole adult life to do that. Sometimes I succeed and sometimes I fail. But when I succeed, I feel happy.

People want to be happy, but they keep trying to "multitask." The truth is that no one can multitask well. Something always gets shortchanged – most likely serenity.

I vote for serenity. Be here now.

[2012]

I don't understand why people carry their cell phones and answer them at all times. Why would anyone wish to be available twenty-four hours a day? As the New Zealanders say, "I can't be bothered."

Part Five
Looking Back

With my brother Danny – 7887 W. Beckett Avenue, circa 1956

She Thought She Was Only Typing

When I was growing up, we had this steel elephant of a manual typewriter. My mother could type a gajillion words a minute. I swear I saw her do this a couple of times: she plunked down the typewriter with a thud, onto the kitchen table. Then she sat and started typing the funniest story, her fingers a blur, the keys going *thunk, thunk.* The words kept pouring out of her head, down her arms, into her fingers, onto the keys and the page. Mum laughed as she wrote the stories, and we laughed when we read them.

Honest to God, I think she just liked to type. Her brother, my Uncle Werner, had the same passion for typing. Uncle Werner lived in a veterans' mental institution in Tomah, Wisconsin. Sometimes when he'd come visit us, he'd sit at the kitchen table with that hulking typewriter in front of him, lay out the morning newspaper on the top of the table, and start typing as if he were taking dictation from the news pages, word for word, fast.

Mum was like that, a sort of unchained typer. I'm positive she thought of herself as "just typing," not writing. She was a daughter, wife, mother of five, cook, cleaner, seamstress, volunteer, but not a writer – except that rather than typing the newspaper or the phone book, she typed incredible impromptu stories. They were fiction, silly, full of puns, about people with funny names, doing outrageous things. I wish I had one copy of one story. I wish I could remember one thing she wrote. All I know is the stories were wildly imaginative, really funny, and short.

I like to think about a mother who wrote hilarious stories in mad freewrites and thought of herself as a typist when really, deep down, she was a writer.
[2006]

This Old House

My old neighborhood is a typical northwest Milwaukee area: houses, stores, taverns, and used car lots on every square inch. But when we moved to 7887 W. Beckett Avenue in 1956, things looked different.

Our house was one of the first built in the neighborhood, and it was a mud lot scene: gravel road, no sidewalks, no lawns. The alley was naked; no gravel, just dust on hot days and mud on rainy ones.

Down the road were big earth mounds and a huge creek. It really looked like "the country." We kids picked wild flowers, sucked the sweet juices out of purple clover blossoms, captured countless turtles, experienced wild fears of quicksand, and tried to nurse an abandoned litter of scrawny black baby rabbits that hadn't yet opened their eyes. Of course they died after a few days – my first experience with death.

Where a funeral home and gas station stand now, there was a field with trees, right next to my best friend Carol LaVesser's house. She and I played in that field for hours and hours, creating our long summer days out of nature and our imaginations. I can still feel the sun on my back when I picture us sitting in those soft, long grasses.

In a few years, that wilderness was gone. We watched our roads and alleys become paved, and sidewalks built. We played on the giant street-building machines, in countless newly-dug basements, in the scoops of the huge steam shovels.

Gradually our "countryside" evolved into a neighborhood.

One thing that never changed, though, was the vacant lot across the street from our house. There was always a "For Sale" sign on it, and no one ever bought it. It became a haven for us as our fields and creeks were replaced by Cape Cods and ranch homes and four-family apartment buildings.

In our vacant lot were a few scraggly trees, long weeds, and one giant billboard. I wasn't big enough to climb the billboard until I was ten or so. Once atop the platform, we had a great view of the cars streaming by, below us, on Appleton Avenue. We had a feeling of power and accomplishment. It was a perfect place for dreaming.

My brother Danny and his "army" friends built forts in the scraggly trees in the shadow of the billboard. That's where they buried the flag I had designed for them with a snake and the words "Don't dread on me."

Summers were great, but we loved our Wisconsin winters, too, and the whole different world they created. On cold, still winter evenings, Danny and I bundled up in our merciless snowsuits that made us walk like robots. We grabbed Pop's old metal-runner sled, and trudged through darkness to the vacant lot. We sledded down the slight incline to the alley. It was fun to be old enough to do that without our parents.

The best part of our old neighborhood was the house I grew up in. I often drive by. I always rubberneck to catch a glimpse of that little white Cape Cod.

My parents turned their tiny city lot into a countrified paradise: a large garden, two big plum trees and a currant bush behind the garage, a beautiful flowering crab in the front yard, and an open feeling with grass and flowers everywhere.

When I was thirteen, my folks sold our house, and the new owners immediately altered that countrified look. They cut down the trees, cemented over the garden, fenced the yard, and installed a backyard pool.

Even with all those changes, I love that house. Once I went back to visit – the owners know me – and I found the house shrunken, which always happens to childhood places we visit as adults. All the 1950s touches were absent, of course: no scratchy chintz chairs and sofa with spiky legs, no garish flowered drapes, no aqua-and-black shower curtain with diamonds and harlequins, no blond bedroom furniture.

But it was still the same house, with its cozy sloped-ceiling upstairs bedroom that always got too hot in summer.

Sometimes I dream about that house. I wake up and realize that in my sleep I've toured the place again and I've bought it. What I plan to do with the home in my dream, I never know.

I really would like to buy that house, because my soul is in it. If ever there were a haunted house, that would be it because it's so full of me – my spirit. I was part of every inch of that place. I never bonded with any other home quite like that again, never felt the love and attachment that I felt for that house when I lived there from age five through thirteen.

I have another fantasy besides buying that place. Right now, a recording studio occupies half of our vacant lot. The other half remains vacant, still impaled with its perpetual "For Sale" sign. The billboard still hovers, plus one scraggly tree. It's as if a spell is cast over that lot – so that no one will ever own it and build on it.

My fantasy is to buy that little hunk of land and turn it into a playground for the neighborhood kids, so they can always enjoy it like I did. I've seen tiny playgrounds like that, and they're well-used. One day I went so far as to call the number on the "For Sale" sign to see how much the lot would cost. Only $35,000! Well, at least I can dream about it.

And whatever happens to our vacant lot, I'll always know that my "Don't dread on me" flag is buried there. Part of me is there, just as I'm still part of that old house where I grew up.

[1982]

The First

Once
during a rainstorm
fierce thunderbolts and
lightning,
I married
the land –
laid myself down on it,
hugged it,
in the vacant lot
on Glendale Street.

I was thirteen then
and the land
will always be
my first
spouse.

[1991]

Of all the farm expressions my mother taught me, my favorite is "stone boat." The stone boat, she explained, was a wagon the farmer pulled in spring as he gathered up frost-heaved stones from his fields. The term "stone boat" became symbolic in our family for anything or anyone that was a burden.

Home Movies

Forty years doesn't seem like so long ago until you watch a home movie from the early 1960s. My parents' home movies are now on videotape, after years of my procrastination, fear of cost, confusion about where to start the project, and misplacing the movies. It seems like a lot of time and effort to find out that I came from the Dark Ages.

Evidence is everywhere in the video that times were much, much different in 1962. Consider these images (all soundless):

Baseball: There's part of a Milwaukee Braves game. And there's a pick-up game at every family gathering, every company picnic, every event where people old and young gather. There's my beautiful mother tossing a ball in the air and cracking it with a bat.

My dad plays badminton with a cigarette hanging from his mouth.

My mom goes to church wearing a big hat, a dress and sunglasses with white plastic frames. My sister and I wear dresses and hats, too. We used to wear short white gloves to church, but they must have been in the wash the day my dad took the movie of us.

We are also dressed up – Mum in high heels, and my dad and brothers wearing ties – when we visit an outdoor shrine somewhere in Wisconsin.

Elsewhere, Mum wears side-zipped pedal pushers.

There are tons of children. The neighborhood is alive with them. It really was the Baby Boom.

There are tons of children, probably around third or fourth grade age, hanging around adults playing croquet. I can't imagine kids doing that today. They'd probably be off by themselves, inside, playing video games.

147

My dad runs alongside my sister as she rides her first two-wheel bike. No need for training wheels.

On a trip to Niagara Falls, our family stops for a picnic in the yard of a Canadian schoolhouse whose cornerstone reads 1856. No fast food.

Cars are big. Our DeSoto has fins. No one is buckled up.

I ride my bike with my little brother David sitting in my bike basket. Neither one of us is wearing a helmet.

My parents, aunts and uncles dance in the basement. They do the Twist and the Bossa Nova.

Everyone, young and old, breaks into the Twist when it looks like they can't think of what to do for the camera.

[2000]

With Pop, Danny, Sally, and David, and DeSoto, circa 1960

First Kisses, and Secrets

I was a little girl, in sixth grade at Our Lady of Sorrows school in Milwaukee, when I first met Hansi. Little did I realize then that he would become the love of my life in a couple of years.

I was standing at the school bus stop, wearing a rummage-sale sailor dress and holding my red-checked schoolbag, when I saw him for the first time. He half-ran to the stop, the wind de-slicking his long blond hair. He grinned – a cockeyed, skinny-faced, friendly smile. "Hello," he said, with a slight foreign accent. Still smiling, he set his bright green eyes upon me. "I am Hansi Fleckenstein. I'm from Austria."

We became good friends during that school year; something about him always made me laugh. Perhaps it was his habit of telling the most ridiculous elephant jokes. But more likely, I giggled a lot because he was an older man, in eighth grade, and always paid particular attention to me. Hansi, who became known as Johnny, was the worst show-off I'd ever seen.

I didn't realize yet why he acted that way in front of me. One winter day at the bus stop, he tried to show me his "Olympic running style." About halfway down the block, at top speed, he slipped on the icy sidewalk and landed smack on his skinny Austrian bottom. Snorting noises burst from my nose as I tried not to laugh.

I told my mother about Johnny's stunts, but she didn't seem amused. With knitted eyebrows, she said, "You know Gail, you're eleven now, and that means having a lot more responsibility." I didn't understand. I didn't know yet that things were changing inside of me, and I think Mum was a little scared about her first daughter growing up.

Mum must've believed that busy girls stay out of mischief. She kept me hopping all summer after sixth grade: ironing, cleaning, and hanging clothes. Throughout the drudgery of tackling dirty bathroom floors and piles of laundry, I daydreamed. Someday my name would be in lights, and I'd escape all this. Judy Garland in the original "A Star is Born" on TV inspired me. I planned marriage to my idol, Edd "Kookie" Byrnes. "Sure he's twenty-four, but he'll wait for me," I told my friend Carol.

Between daydreams, I babysat for the neighbors. Mum's idea of "more responsibility" included having a steady job, and she got one for me at the Polachecks', down the block. I took care of their four kids each Friday evening – for fifty cents an hour. I was getting used to my weekly earnings of two dollars and fifty cents when I made a surprising discovery: Johnny Fleckenstein lived next door to the Polachecks.

I was teaching the Polacheck kids the art of cutting paper dolls when the doorbell rang one night. I answered it, and there he was, grinning that familiar wide smile.

"Hello," he said. "Sometimes I come over to play with the kids – I don't have any little brothers or sisters."

It became ritual for Johnny to visit Randy, Kathy, Peggy, and Mary Jo Polacheck – and me – each Friday. Mum had told me never to let boys into a house while I babysat, but Mrs. Polacheck didn't mind. She liked Johnny (and I didn't mind his company, either). Mum decided to let her "no boys" rule bend a little in this special case. So Johnny and I became Mommy and Daddy on Fridays to the Polacheck kids.

I was amazed at how nice Johnny was to me. He sure was more helpful than my brother Danny. One night after supper, he grabbed a dish towel while I was washing dishes. I cocked my head and said, "I thought boys didn't like to do dishes."

"Well, once in a while isn't too bad," he answered, smiling. He looked away quickly and changed the subject with, "Why do elephants sleep with their legs straight up in the air?"

I shrugged my shoulders.

"To trip birds!" he exclaimed with a wink, and I groaned. I gave him a swat with the soggy dish rag, and he fwapped me with the towel.

The faithful two dollars and fifty cents rolled in each week all through that summer and into the next school year. Now I was a seventh-grader, and Johnny was a big freshman at John Marshall High. The "West Side Story" hood look was *in* and he apparently thought he was elite with his black clothes and Cuban-heeled, pointy-toed shoes. He ignored me, and he stopped showing up on Friday nights at the Polachecks'.

But it didn't bother me. Mum always said "There are plenty of fish in the sea," and there were a lot of boys at Our Lady of Sorrows elementary, where I went to school. I wasn't "hooked" on Johnny yet, and I emerged triumphantly as one of the social queens at the completion of seventh grade.

I found myself spending more and more time in front of the mirror; those things that were changing inside of me were beginning to show on the outside. My face was getting thinner, but I was getting rounder in feminine places. My rummage-sale sailor dress had long been put away in the attic for the time when my little sister Sally could wear it. Through Girl Scouts, I received a book entitled *You're a Young Lady Now* that catalogued the mysteries of menstruation and sanitary napkins. I kept the book safely in my underwear drawer so my brother Danny wouldn't find it.

I was twelve years old, and I was bursting with feelings that welled up from deep inside me.

Sometimes it hurt so much to keep the feelings inside that I started writing stories, poems, and a diary (filled with passages about my weekly-changing crushes). I never locked the diary, because I knew Mum didn't snoop; I simply placed it in my desk drawer after writing in it each night.

One evening I wrote a poem about Johnny and two boys I liked at O.L.S. It was called "Whom Shall I Kiss Tonight?" and I put it to music on the piano. I hid the poem in my underwear drawer so Mum wouldn't see it even by accident. There were certain things I didn't feel comfortable sharing with her anymore.

My wallet thickened regularly each Friday throughout the school year at the Polachecks' house. June brought the pleasant possibility of seeing Johnny again (even though I didn't want to admit to myself that I missed him).

The first time I heard the doorbell ring on a Friday night was in mid-June, and I felt a somersault low in my stomach. Forcing myself to be "cool," I had little Mary Jo answer it. She let Johnny in, and when I saw his face again, I couldn't suppress a great smile and a most cheerful, "Well, hi, it's good to see you again!"

Before he even said hello, Johnny reached into his back pocket and whipped out a mini-camera (about three inches by three inches – they were a fad). He snapped a button and caught me on film.

"I got a new camera," he said with a grin, "and I had to try it out on a good subject." I was too flattered and flabbergasted to think what a corny line that was.

I put the kids to bed a lot more cheerfully than usual that night. Even a Kookie Byrnes movie on T.V. couldn't keep my thoughts off Johnny. He had changed a lot during the past year. His arms were muscular (I noticed them bulging beneath the rolled-up sleeves of his white tee shirt). His voice was even deeper than before. But most devastating was the fact that his green eyes were even more warm and sparkling than ever, and I felt engulfed in them. I was hooked.

Johnny was fifteen now, an established teenager – it would be four months till I would enter *my* teens. But our age difference didn't bother Johnny and me. We were still great friends and loved to babysit together, even though I wouldn't run races with him anymore or jump rope with the Polacheck kids. I felt too Jell-O-y to do those things in front of Johnny now.

July came. Johnny started visiting me at my house, usually on the pretense of talking with my eleven-year-old brother Danny. After ditching my pesky little brother, we went off and did most anything we felt like. We sat on the grass under the flowering crab tree in the front yard and played with my little black mutt Corky; Johnny fixed my bike and washed his greasy hands in the set tub in my family's basement laundry room (I felt embarrassed because some of my dirty underwear was lying around down there); we climbed the billboard in the vacant lot across the street.

One day after we'd been billboard-scaling, Mum took me aside. "Watch out for him," she warned. "I think he's sweet on you."

I tried to look astonished, opening my eyes wide. "Don't worry, Mum, John and I are just buds."

The next day when Johnny and I were walking together down the alley, Billy Baron and Randy Potter whined, "John li-ikes Gail, John li-ikes Gail." Johnny picked up some pebbles and threw them at the boys. Then he grabbed my hand and we ran all the way down the alley, laughing. When we finally stopped for breath, Johnny looked down at me and grinned. My face got hot and I pulled my hand out of his.

One Friday night shortly after that day, Johnny became bolder – but I was still gutless. He and I had put the Polacheck kids to bed, and we were living-room bound when he stopped me in the dark, quiet bedroom hallway. He put his arm in front of me, his hand against the wall. Blocking my path, he stared at me with those intense green eyes. I giggled, ducked under his arm, ran into the living room, and turned on the T.V. I felt afraid, although I wanted to be close to him more than anything.

August sizzled in, and I grew more and more aware that soon my Austrian friend would be going off to John Marshall High again, and I to O.L.S. The two schools were across the street from each other, but I'd never see Johnny during the school year, if last year was any indication. Johnny was really getting old now. He'd be a sophomore that year. So I made the best of the time that I had with him.

I forgot everything – writing, chores, worrying – except for Johnny, during those sunny days. I daydreamed about him constantly, and at night I'd go for long lonely quiet walks with my dog Corky. I softly sang "Johnny Angel" as I strolled. My fantasies blossomed. I took some old paraffin from a jar of Mum's homemade jelly and shaped a set of lips out of it. I stuck the lips on my bedroom wall, about the right height for Johnny's lips. Each night before bed I kissed those wax lips, long, lingering, and lovingly.

Then on a middle-of-August warm Friday evening, it happened. Johnny and I were playing outside with the Polacheck kids when we caught a basketball at the same time. I wouldn't let go; neither would he. He was quite strong, and he dragged me into the house by the basketball, telling Randy and Kathy and Peggy and Mary Jo, "I have to have a talk with Gail." The kids ignored us and kept playing.

I put up a slight (very slight) struggle, but I never let go of the basketball, and Johnny pulled me through the hallway and into the bathroom. It was black as my dog Corky in there; there was no window. Johnny closed the door and I could hear the "click" when he locked it. I tried to say something, but he pushed me back against the cold tile wall. I tripped backwards up onto the bathroom scale. The scale went BRRRRROOOOIIINNNNGGGG! and we dropped the basketball. For a second I was scared, for Johnny was strong, and Mum had given me warnings. I gulped loudly. But Johnny was gentle as he put his hands on the sides of my face and tilted my head first to the left, then to the right.

Then he kissed me on the lips for maybe five seconds, and ran out of the room

I was in a daze – my first kiss! How long had I wondered what it would be like? And now The Moment had passed. But not for long.

Johnny came back for seconds that same night. He took me into the bathroom to "have another talk." This time he kissed me five long, soft times. All the while, my palms grew sweaty and I was sure my aim would be off. Everything inside me was pounding. I was too afraid to do anything but let my arms hang at my sides and say (dramatically, I thought), "Oh, Johnny!"

Then Johnny was gone. But I could still feel the warmth of his hands on my face and the damp of his kisses on my lips. I smiled when I put the kids to bed, and I smiled when Mr. and Mrs. Polacheck came home. I couldn't stop smiling – the muscles in my cheeks were becoming sore – and I thought sure that the Polachecks would notice I was acting weird. But they didn't say a word; they gave me my usual two dollars and fifty cents, and I put it, tremble-fingered, into my wallet.

After I walked back to my house, there was Mum, putting together a jigsaw puzzle like nothing had happened. I smiled my goofy grin at her too, murmuring "Hi – pretty nice night out, hey?"

Mum looked up, saying, "I don't know – I've been inside."

She didn't notice.

I was hurting with the joy. I wanted to share it with Mum – or anyone – but I couldn't tell her. I turned from my mother and bounded up the stairs to my room. I let my joy pour into my diary and then carefully locked it for the first time. I hid it in the drawer along with my "Whom Shall I Kiss Tonight?" poem.

I could feel my face still irrepressibly smiling. The corners of my mouth seemed to stretch to my earlobes. I never imagined I'd get my first kiss on a bathroom scale, but I *had* hoped it would be from Johnny. I put on my nightie and lay for a long time on my bed in the darkness, warm, and smiling. I felt strange – almost glowing – yet *Mum hadn't guessed.*

That's how I remember it. A first kiss on a bathroom scale: silly. A few gentle moments: nice.

And something more: the start of a part of my life that always remained special, secret, my own.

[1968, with thanks to BCHS creative writing teacher Diane Doerfler]

I wear an inside-out sweatshirt. A young person calls me on it. I say, "That's what cool people wear." I don't add, "in 1965."

Walking to the Shower Wearing Socks

It was September 1964. I was thirteen years old. It was my first day of gym class. And I was terrified.

It was my second day as a freshman at Brookfield Central High School, and it hadn't been too good so far. I was new in town. I knew only one girl in the whole school, Kathi Yeko, my childhood friend. I was navigationally challenged. I had gotten lost fourteen times yesterday.

We had five minutes between classes and I was always holding all these big heavy books in my arms plus my purse over my shoulder, and when I finally got to my locker, it took me six or seven tries to work my locker combination:

Clear it. Right to thirty-nine. Left past zero to eleven. Right to twenty-two.

Clear it. Right to thirty-nine, left past zero to eleven, right to twenty-two.

Clear it. Right to thirty nine, left past zero to eleven, right to twenty-two. And I was sweating all over my forehead.

Gym class would be third hour today and I'd only gotten lost in the halls four times, so I was doing better than yesterday.

But – *gym class*! Or as they said at Brookfield Central, *Phy Ed.*

Phy Ed! It sounded harsh. I was terrified.

I didn't think of myself as athletic, or even coordinated. We never had gym class at Our Lady of Sorrows grade school in Milwaukee. The closest I got to physical activity there was dancing the cha cha and the polka on the playground with my best friend Carol.

I did ride my bike when I was sure I wouldn't bump into anyone I knew, and I played the occasional game of dodge ball or softball at family reunions, but I thought of myself as a klutz.

However, that's not why I was terrified. I was scared because of the locker room. I was terrified because I knew I'd have to get naked in front of a bunch of strangers.

Anyway, the start of gym class wasn't too bad. We had three minutes to change for class. I found my assigned gym locker, fiddled with yet another combination – only three times. There were a couple of quiet freshman girls near me and a bunch of sophomore girls at the end of the bench in my aisle, chattering away. It seemed that nobody saw me, which was fine.

I shoved my books and my purse into the locker. I whipped off my plaid skirt and my white blouse with the Peter Pan collar, threw them in. I pulled off my brown loafers and bobby sox and threw them in too, I snuck a look at the sophomore girls. Peroxide-blonde pageboys, peroxide-blonde flips.

I put on my gym uniform – royal blue cotton shorts and a white cotton button-up blouse my mom had ironed. I pulled on my gym socks and white tennis shoes, and off I went into the gym to the freshman side. Our teacher, Miss W., was kindly and old and had the exact same body as the sophomore's teacher, Miss S., who was much younger. They both had efficient legs and short hair.

Miss W. led us in calisthenics and told us we were going to learn ball-handling skills next class. Oh boy. She spent a lot of time going over the rules of Phy Ed class, including *Be on time* and *Take a full soapy shower* and *Prove it by showing your wet bare butt to Miss S.*, who will hand you a towel. The big shower room was for everyone to use. The little room with the curtain was for our special time of month.

Gym class was over, and Miss W. said we had seven minutes to take our shower and change back to regular clothes. *Seven minutes*! Now I was terrified *and* in a rush! I could feel the sweat getting ready to pop out on my forehead.

I trooped back to my locker room aisle. I fiddled with the locker combination again, twice this time, whipped off my blouse and shorts and threw them in the locker. I kicked off my tennies and shoved them under the bench. The blondes were talking and giggling down the bench. I had less than seven minutes.

I looked down at my white cotton size 32A bra. The fabric was all puckered where I did not fill it in. I took a breath and pushed down the straps, whipped the bra around, unhooked it and flung it into the locker. I had less than seven minutes.

I took another breath. The sophomores were still cackling away. I snuck a peek. Whoa. One of them had gigantic jiggling boobs and *pink* bikini underpants. I'd never seen anything like that.

I looked down at my very substantial white cotton underpants and in one stroke, whipped them off and flung them into the locker.

There I was, all ninety-eight pounds of me.

The room was chilly. I had less than seven minutes. The sweat was starting to coat my forehead, and it felt clammy now. I walked toward the peroxide girls, toward the shower room, averting my eyes, eager for the cover soon to be provided by the towel Miss S. would hand me (I didn't realize yet that the towel would be miniscule and have very little absorbency).

I was almost past the blonde flips and page-boys when I heard a loud voice followed by a clutch of cackles: "Look! She's wearing her socks to the shower!"

I looked down. Yup. Those were my two feet, and white socks were on them.

I retraced my steps, flung those stupid white socks under the bench, then zipped now blindly through those mean cackling hens, to the shower. I don't remember anything else about that experience, but I'm sure I made it in my allotted seven minutes.

I learned two things that morning that I've never forgotten:

1. You don't need to make people feel bad when they've made mistakes. They already feel bad.

2. Never wear socks to the shower.

[2006, with thanks to UWM storytelling teacher John McGivern]

Mr. Velguth, a teacher at Brookfield Central High School, always said, "Learn everything you can about any job." Recently my grandson Oliver and I spent a half-hour watching Alterra bakers make cinnamon rolls: fascinating!

My Torture of a Little Brother

I was the oldest child, which means I was the bossiest child. Sally, David, and George were much younger. They existed to serve me. Danny, however, was another story. Danny was my torture of a little brother. He first intruded on my life when I was two years old. Before Danny, things were quiet. My mother would set me on her lap and read to me. We took long naps together every afternoon. Papa would hoist me onto his shoulders and hop on his bike. We rode to the pond down the road, where he fished with rod and reel and I fished with stick and string.

When Danny came, everything changed. He wouldn't take naps. Danny climbed on every piece of furniture we had. He fell off every piece of furniture we had. He climbed up steps. He fell down steps. As soon as he could walk, he ran. When he was big enough, he ran across our bedroom and leaped to dive-bomb his bed, hollering "Cowabunga!" He missed the bed. His face was full of Band-Aids and scars.

I tried to be his friend. I shared my bedroom with him. I gave him rides on my tricycle. We dressed up in old clothes and put on shows for our parents. We got lost in my grandmother's woods together. Our mom called us "Hansel and Gretel." I told Danny the story of "Sleeping Beauty" every night before we went to sleep.

But Danny made it his job to torment me. One of his favorite games of torture was The Typewriter. I'd be quietly lying on my stomach on the living room floor, watching "Captain Kangaroo." Dancing Bear would be dancing around – and around – and around – to a really long song. Danny wasn't interested in Dancing Bear. With no warning, he'd flip me over onto my back, and then he'd sit on me, typing his fingers into my belly. With a big, sick smile on his face.

161

I'd tell him to stop, but then The Typewriter would turn into The Echo.

"Stop it!" I'd shout.

"Stop it" Danny would echo, still typing, with that sickeningly sweet smile on his face.

"I'm not kidding – leave me alone!" (me)

"I'm not kidding – leave me alone!" (him)

And on and on.

As we grew into older elementary school children at Our Lady of Sorrows, our fights grew in fervor. I can't remember what any of our battles were about, but they always involved wrestling. We beat each other up. I know there will never be world peace because I have felt murder lust coursing through my veins. I have said "I could kill you!' to Danny, and meant it. I could taste it. It tasted good.

I had a particular wrestling hold that brought Danny down. I looped my arm around his neck, pulled hard, and slammed him right down – like that! *Boom.* Got him every time. It was great to be bigger and stronger.

During summer vacations, Danny and I had brief periods of *détente* in our ongoing war. He had a gang of buddies that roamed our neighborhood on bicycles – Mike Delaney, Denny Stauber, Randy Potter, and sometimes the Schneider kids from down the alley. They all wore crew cuts, dungarees, and PF Flyers. They played "War" with finger machine guns and a lot of spit. They fought in the vacant lot across the street from our house, on the corner of Glendale and Appleton Avenues in Milwaukee. They made forts in the scrubby trees and bushes there. Occasionally they asked me and Peggy Potter, the girl across the street, to be their nurses. The garage was our hospital. The boys came to the hospital after skirmishes so Peggy and I could operate on them. I didn't understand then the strange thrill I got from bandaging those wounded soldiers.

One day Danny asked me to make him a flag. He must have got the idea from a history book he remembered from school. He told me the design he wanted on the flag: a coiled snake with its head ready to strike, and the words "Don't dread on me."

I got an old white pillowcase from our mom, and my box of crayons – "magic markers" hadn't yet been invented. That evening, I drew a coiled snake with its head ready to strike, and the words "Don't dread on me" on the pillowcase. It was hard drawing with crayons on cloth because the cloth kept wiggling and I had to press so hard with the crayons. I worked for a long, long time.

The next day, I presented the flag to Danny and his gang. They smiled, grabbed the flag, and ran off to the vacant lot. I felt proud.

That night I asked Danny where the flag was.

"We burned it and buried it in the vacant lot," he said, blasé, "like a real war flag."

"You *burned it* – and *buried it*?"

"Yeah, like in a real war."

"I could *kill* you!"

As we grew into teenager-hood, Danny became Dan. His adventures became bolder because he wasn't afraid of anything. I could slalom water-ski, but Dan could water-ski on a canoe paddle, making a giant rooster tail of water behind him because he leaned way over, with his shoulder almost touching the lake surface. He wasn't afraid to fall. Even though he's almost three years younger than I am, he did everything before me – and before it was legal – including driving, smoking, and drinking.

We no longer shared a bedroom, but his bedroom was right under mine. He played his music loud. I'd be trying to read or study and he'd be playing "Tommy" for the hundredth time. I'd jump up as high as I could and come down *bang* on my bedroom floor, like a

163

bomb, to give him the message to *shut up*! It didn't help. I couldn't beat him up anymore, but I still felt the blood lust – I felt it inside of me: *I could kill him.*

I was seventeen when it occurred to me that Dan and I could be friends. My boyfriend Jim Price was best friends with his sister Lori. They shared secrets. So I started talking to Dan. We played hooky from Sunday Mass together, driving out to the moors and creeks of Brookfield, talking.

When Dan was a college freshman, he had a fight with my dad. Dan left home and said he wouldn't be back. Mum was crying. Pop didn't know what to do. I still lived at home and I knew approximately where Dan had fled – a rough area west of Marquette High in Milwaukee. Without saying anything to my parents, I got in my Ford Pinto and went to look for Dan. It was dark and I was scared wandering through that neighborhood, but I finally found him – playing guitar in the basement of his friend's house. I knocked on the basement window and he came out.

I kind of whispered, "Dan, you gotta come home and talk to Mum. She's crying."

Dan came home with me. He went right to Mum.

Pop came to me. He was really hot, and red in the face, and he was crying. He hugged me and said, "Thank you, Gail."

Once, when we were in our thirties, I asked Dan if he remembered that wrestling hold I used to bring him down in the old days. "Remember? It went like this," I said, looping my arm around his neck. I pulled on his neck like I used to, but Dan didn't budge.

Then with one arm, he picked me up. There we were, laughing, me hanging in the air with my arm still looped around his neck.

"I could kill you," I said, smiling.

"I could kill you," he echoed, smiling too.
[2006, with thanks to UWM storytelling teacher John McGivern]

164

The Departure of "The Quiet One"

I woke up on November 30 and had no idea George Harrison was dead. I was doing floor exercises in front of the television when the newsman told me George was gone. I froze mid-leg lift, like a ten-year-old playing "Statue Maker." I couldn't do another leg lift because my whole body was shaking with sobs.

I didn't know a thirteen-year-old girl remained inside me. That's how old I was when I fell in love with George Harrison.

I was thirteen in September 1964 when I went to see the Beatles perform in Milwaukee. My ticket for the best seat in the Arena cost $5.50 – eleven hours of my labor babysitting.

I was thirteen when I fashioned a pair of lips from my mom's canning paraffin, stuck the lips high on my bedroom wall, and practiced kissing them. They were George's lips (most of the time; sometimes they belonged to one of the boys I was currently in love with).

It was that thirteen-year-old girl who was crying like a ninny on the floor that Friday morning.

The radio and television droned on with tributes: What a musician he was.

Great guitarist.

Super songwriter.

Overshadowed by John and Paul.

Never wanted to be a fireman, only wanted to be in a band.

The Quiet One. Never wanted fame.

Pioneer of charity with Concert for Bangladesh.

They missed the point. We Beatlemaniacs who loved George didn't love him for any of those reasons. We loved George because he was *George*. Any thirteen-year-old girl could look into those eyes and see his depth of soul.

He was, indeed, the quiet one. Some of us who loved George grew up to marry quiet men.

Those who loved Paul preferred "cute," bubbly boys like the cheerleader-type McCartney.

Those who loved John Lennon, the "serious one," gravitated toward intellectuals later in life.

Ringo Starr-lovers? Maybe they liked clowns or severe underdogs.

Only recently had I noticed George's name in the news. I knew that a crazed man broke into his home and stabbed him repeatedly. I knew George had been fighting cancer for years. I wondered how many cigs he had smoked.

But I hadn't thought about George for decades. I hadn't even prayed for his health when I learned he was ailing. I heard his songs on the radio that Friday, and I realized that I never knew he wrote half of them.

But when I learned that his gentle spirit left this earth, it shook me to my soul.

[2001]

*"Character and personality are two different things." –
Edna McGrath Grenier, my grandmother "Mémère."*

Part Six
Keeping Traditions

With Danny and Sally and '53 Ford, circa 1959, Milwaukee area
– next to plowed snowbank towering over our heads

My Secret Park

We'd been on the road forty minutes and I'd drifted into wonderful travel slumber. We were close to Riveredge Nature Center in little Newburg, near the Washington/Ozaukee County line, when suddenly my husband said, "That's a pretty park."

I opened my eyes and, in the second that I had to glance out before we passed by, I *knew*. "Mike! Mike!" I said. "That's the triangle park! Oh my god! Stop the car!"

I was sitting straight up, gesturing, shaken from my drowsiness. Mike pulled into a parking lot adjoining the grassy triangle. The kids were already editorializing:

Charlie said, "Have a cow, Mom."

Brian accused, "You said, 'Oh my god!'"

Anna said, "Jeeze, Louise!"

Mike turned off the car. We sat there and I stared. I was looking directly into the answer to a question that had bothered me for years: Where is our secret park?

The place had been the scene of unique pleasure for this city kid, and over the years I've dragged my husband down many a remote road searching for it, always in vain. Now we had stumbled onto it, quite by accident, and the park was a mystery no longer. As I sat motionless in the car, images from the past danced through my head ....

The cheapest I can remember the price of gas is nineteen cents a gallon, and my park memories go back a long time before that. It was during that era when Milwaukee families like ours would take drives into the country on pleasant Sundays after church.

Our family's special site was a triangle-shaped patch of grass formed by several roads, farm land all around.

Mum used to complain that my nose was always in a book and I never enjoyed the scenery, and I'm sure that's why I never got a sense of where we drove. But once we got there, the park belonged to us alone, and I abandoned the book back in the car.

We three kids (like my children now) were more interested in running around than in a picnic lunch. Two sides of the triangle were lined with rows of trees, which gave us endless opportunities for hide-and-seek.

But by far the best thing about our secret park was the three-legged goat that lived across the road. Although she was separated from us by a barbed wire fence, she was friendly, and we spent a lot of time petting her. The most exotic animal we'd ever touched was a cat, so the goat was a big thrill.

Times change, gas prices rise, people grow up. My parents died before I thought to ask them where that park was. So I wondered, I reminisced about the three-legged goat, and I told my husband how much I'd like to find that place.

On Mother's Day, my vote holds the most weight, and our family goes where I decide. This year, it was Riveredge Nature Center in Newburg. I had never been there but had heard it was terrific.

We packed our three children in the back seat and took off. I never expected the Mother's Day bonus of finding my secret park. I relished the experience, although the place has changed greatly. The trees that frame it have grown huge. Where it once was empty and seemed to be unknown to all but my family, it now holds ten redwood-stained picnic tables.

A sign proclaims: "Private Park. For No No's Customers Only." Sure enough, a restaurant/bar sat on the other side of the parking lot.

I looked across the road to the south. No barbed wire, no goat, only acres and acres of land at rest. Across the other road were modern-looking ranch homes.

I don't cry easily, but I started to blubber. Not because it wasn't the boondocks anymore. Not because it was "Private." But because there was no one to ask about it.

It was Mother's Day *and* my mother's birthday, and I couldn't ask her. I couldn't ask my dad, either. So I cried. Sometimes it doesn't feel good to be the oldest one left in the family.

Mike and the kids waited silently. I never got out of the car and, after a few minutes, we drove north to Riveredge. We hiked all around the nature center, saw birds we'd never seen before, and got sunburned.

Charlie and Brian held my hands, something they haven't done in – I can't remember how long. Maybe it was their way of wordlessly comforting me for an ache they couldn't understand.

Mike quietly said, "I hope seeing that park didn't wreck your day."

"It *made* my day," I assured him.

A good friend says parents are memory makers, and she's right. I was lucky that my parents made mostly good memories for me. That's why a cherished place from my childhood may change, but it remains the same in my heart. Now I'm a memory maker for my children. Maybe someday Riveredge will be a secret park for them.

[1988]

For our 41st anniversary, Mike and I talked about taking a paddleboard lesson on Green Lake, but wound up going to a movie in Beaver Dam instead. Movie addiction is a strong force. So is laziness.

The First Annual Do-Nothing Day

Wisconsin people are a hardy bunch; it takes *big snow* to keep them home from work. There's a lot of stubborn pride concerning fast and clean sidewalk shoveling and skillful driving through ice and slush.

In thirty years of coping with Wisconsin winters, I've never seen a day like Tuesday, December 15, 1987. I have childhood photos of snowdrifts twice as tall as cars. But never in my adult life have I experienced non-delivery from both the U.S. Postal Service and the *Milwaukee Journal.*

During a record-breaking twenty-four-hour period, we were pounded and pelted with more than a foot of the wettest of all wet snows. Winds whooped all day, at almost hurricane force. And an amazing thing: during the blizzard we were rattled and ripped by thunder and lightning. I've seen those only during rain storms. The inferno was doubly shocking after two months of pussy-footing around by Mom Nature: we had one snow that didn't stick in October and one that stuck for only a couple of days in November. Suddenly, with a real blizzard, Canada geese that had been hanging around "on the fence" high-tailed it south.

At our house, the day started out quite routinely. We knew the night before that a storm was coming, but we Wisconsinites get blasé about those things. My husband rolled out of bed at 6:00 a.m., pushed the drapes aside, peeked out and saw that the window was solid white with driven snow. His only comment was a mumbled "Wow." Then he trudged to the bathroom and immersed himself, as usual, in a hot bath.

While Mike soaked, I got two phone calls from his co-workers, who had been listening to the radio's ominous weather reports and zillion school and business closings. The bottom line was: no school or work today.

I brought Mike this news bulletin (there was no way I was going to fall back to sleep) as he lay surrounded by bubbles. His response was, "I'm goin' in. I have to."

"No way!" I protested. "You're not gonna risk your neck to get to work!" But I knew that if he could, he would. I left him there with his bubbles and his *Forbes*.

Our sixth-grade son Charlie was already up, trying to finish some homework he hadn't completed the evening before. He was a bit more enthusiastic than Mike was about the prospect of a day off. "Yippee!" he shouted, slamming down his pencil and making a bee-line for our big cozy bed with its electric blanket. His three-year-old sister Anna and nine-year-old brother Brian were still sawing logs upstairs. It didn't take Charlie long to re-enter the Land of Nod.

As it turned out, Mike's fierce determination to punch clock was for naught. Our long, steep, curved driveway was impassable. So, exactly ten days before Christmas, smack in the midst of pre-holiday chaos, our family got an unplanned vacation together. Now that it's over, I think the President should declare Do-Nothing Day a national holiday on December 15. All stores, banks, schools, businesses, and factories would *have* to close.

Our day was a perfectly wonderful day full of things we hadn't had time to do. We spent some time together and some time in little clusters. Occasionally we were energetic and often we were deliciously lazy. There was cartoon watching, Sunday newspaper reading, snowman making, snow shoveling, snow tasting, and card playing. Two friends called to see how I was enjoying the day and one called on business because she knew she'd catch me at home (for a change).

When I realized we'd have a day together, my first thought was "Great! Now Mike can fix the cookie press and we'll make some cookies." We were part of a 4-H cookie exchange, and I had agreed to provide twelve dozen spritz cookies by the following Saturday evening. By that Tuesday, Brian and I had made about four dozen beautiful ones and about eight dozen mechanically-induced pitiful failures (which we promptly ate). It was becoming too fattening to go on in that way.

However, the cookies never got baked that day. Other more important things were accomplished – like folding six baskets of laundry. And, after two hours of talking about it, Mike dragged the Christmas tree in from where it had been standing outside, full of snow. It left great puddles in the front hall. We all worked to set the tree in its stand and position and re-position it until it was in the perfect place, hogging half the living room. "It looks weird there," Charlie noted.

"Don't worry," I assured him. "You'll get used to it."

Afterward (such jobs are tiring), Mike and Anna and I snuggled in for a long nap. Before retiring, I warned the boys: "No TV! No cookies! No fighting and no noise!" We slept like rocks, the wind whooshing outside all the while. Storms make great sleeping weather.

Anna was the first to awake. Mike and I were still groggy when the boys started pushing and pulling us out of the sack. Soon we discovered the reason they were so eager for us to get vertical: while we slept, they had decorated our (newly-washed) windows with stick-on Christmas figures. Oh boy! Even more impressive, they had strung the lights onto the Christmas tree.

The tree wasn't a giant, but it was much taller than our sons. I whispered to Mike, "How do you think they got those lights to the top of the tree?"

"I don't know," Mike answered, "and I don't think I want to know."

Somehow with the lights up, we mustered the energy to decorate the tree. Anna, as usual, hung her twenty or so ornaments on a six-inch strand of wire from the tree lights, one foot off the floor. The boys spent some time arguing about who had or had not broken a certain ornament last year. They were probably in fallout from not arguing the whole time Mike and I napped. Charlie continued to insist that "ornament" should be pronounced "or-da-ment."

When we realized that the tree could not hold another trinket, we moseyed into the kitchen and somehow all ended up dancing to our new reggae tape. Suddenly I had a great inspiration to have a Jamaica party in January, to fight off the winter blahs.

"All we'd have to do," I explained to Mike, "is move the kitchen table and chairs out, put down a two-by-four frame on the floor, and fill it with sand. We could dance in it barefoot."

"Like a big sandbox," he said.

"Yeah," I agreed. "And we could make some pretend palm trees and we could stoke up the woodstove so everybody could wear shorts."

Actually, we'd been feeding both the fireplace *and* the woodstove all day to keep out the cold, and the house was toasty. That fact, along with the music and dancing, may have accounted for such a strange inspiration.

Before we turned in for the night, the snowplow man dug us out, Mike took another nap, we turned leftover chili into spaghetti, and we hung up the wet coats to dry.

It was a perfectly wonderful blizzard, for us. And if the President won't enact an Annual Do-Nothing Day, maybe God will.

[1988]

How do little boys know how to make car noises before they turn two years old?

The Blue Dish

I was living in the eye of an emotional hurricane the day I stumbled upon the blue dish.

A young cousin lay in a hospital bed, in critical condition. Great-grandma was undergoing chemotherapy. Two long-married couples, old friends, had separated. Under our own roof, my husband of twenty-three years was struggling through a midlife funk that seemed endless. Mike, my steady, easygoing mate, was having an affair with the blues.

But life goes on, even in the eye of a hurricane. And so it was that on a brisk bright-colored autumn Saturday, Mike and I spent a half-hour strolling through "A Country Affair," an annual antique and craft show in Menomonee Falls. We meandered, laughing about the fact that wooden and metal toys from our youth are now collectibles. Suddenly we turned a corner and almost bumped into the dishes.

"Mike! Those are the dishes I grew up with!"

There they were, loud as ever: the heavy, high-gloss ceramic plates my family used each day during the 1950s. Every plate had a different color glaze: orange, green, gold, mauve, grey, and blue.

Blue.

"Mike! Look! That's the blue dish my brother and I used to fight over!"

"I don't remember that story," Mike said.

I lifted the plate and ran my fingers over it. "Every night at suppertime, Dan and I argued over who got the blue dish. There was only one in the set."

As I looked over the colors of the other plates, I could see why we competed for the blue; it was deep and clear. The other colors were dark and murky, as if true color had been mixed with depression.

Right away, I decided to buy the blue dish for my brother. Wouldn't he get a kick out of having it, without fighting me for it, after all these years! Mike stood quietly beside me while I hatched my plan. He wore the look on his face that said *I know there's no stopping you.*

The price marked on the plate read fifteen dollars. There were actually *two* blue dishes for sale. I studied them and picked the one with fewer knife scuffs for my brother's gift. When I paid my fifteen dollars, I asked the seller to tell me about the dinnerware.

"They're Fiesta dishes," she explained. "They were made from the 1920s to the 1940s."

She quietly wrapped my purchase in tissue paper. I watched her hands at work and felt myself flooded with memories of Dan back when we were growing up on the corner of Beckett and Glendale in Milwaukee .....

He was Danny back then. I was the big sister and he was the little brother. Danny and I fought a lot, and I usually won. I had an excellent neck hold that brought him down every time.

Danny wore a crew-cut every day of his childhood. From the side, in silhouette, his head and neck formed the shape of a question mark. I spent a lot of time staring at that perfect question mark. We did everything together.

Danny wore dungarees, even on the hottest summer days. He built forts and played army and attracted trouble. He was a clown and a dreamer. One time Pop got home from work and saw a tree branch stuck into our gravel driveway. "What's that?" he asked Danny.

"I planted a money tree," Danny explained.

Three more kids joined our family, but there was only one Danny – only one with quite the dreams and quite the knack for trouble. Only one who made me laugh so hard.

Dan lives in California now. He's the brother I rarely talk to and more rarely see. Some time ago, he was mad at me for about three years. He spoke to me, but he didn't *talk*. Somehow we got around that deadfall without really working it through. I still don't know why he was angry. Dan doesn't talk to me about sad stuff. He'd rather make me laugh.

When I get a hug from Dan, he holds on. I know what he's doing: he's waiting until he's sure he can feel my heartbeat. Then he lets go. Whenever we end our infrequent long-distance phone conversations, Dan says, "I love you, big sister." When he calls me big sister, I feel like I just found the blue dish.

I walked away from the antique booth smiling and clutching the blue dish close to me.

That night, the Fiestaware must have worked on me in my dreams. I awoke Sunday morning with the desire for a blue dish of my own. I knew it was silly. What could a blue dish do? It couldn't heal Mike's cousin or cure Great-grandma. It wouldn't mend our friends' marriages. It couldn't lessen Mike's sadness or make him easier to live with. Yet I woke sure that everybody deserves a blue dish, including me.

I knew the antique show ran all weekend, so that morning I said to Mike, "You know, maybe I should buy that other blue dish for myself." Mike didn't say anything. I've become used to his husbandly selective deafness, so I thought nothing of it.

It was a busy Sunday, with both of us buzzing in our separate directions. Around 3:00 pm, I finally got myself to the Fiestaware booth at the antique show. My blue dish was gone. The rest of the plates sat there, stacked in all their ugly orange, green, gold, mauve, and greyness. But there was no clear, bold, dark blue like the one I loved and fought for in my childhood.

Well, I thought, *you lose some.*

That evening I told Mike the story of the phantom blue dish, and he couldn't hold his secret. He burst into a smile. "I bought it," he said. His husbandly selective deafness hadn't been in force after all. While I sat stunned, he ran upstairs to the attic and came back with a dish-sized box, already wrapped: a present for my birthday that was to come in two weeks. I gave him a big hug, unwrapped the dish and propped it on the windowsill in front of the kitchen sink.

That night in bed, Mike and I talked. "I feel like an old collector item," he said.

"No," I said, "you're not old enough. You're a period piece."

Sometimes I have a hard time convincing him that whatever inner storms he faces, I'll stick around until we're both antiques. He weathered my midlife turmoil a few years back, when the world seemed like true color muddied with depression.

Today I'll dig through the catastrophe of my attic for some materials to package Dan's blue dish. I'm going to send it with no note, just my return address. I keep picturing his surprised face. Will he remember the significance of an old blue Fiesta plate? I hope so. He's weathered his share of emotional hurricanes for the past few years. I know the blue dish won't calm the gusts in his world. It won't grow him a money tree. Life will remain the question mark that it has always been. The blue dish is simply a long-distance lingering hug that listens for a heartbeat.

[1995]

"Habit never rests."
  – Edna McGrath Grenier, my Grandmother "Mémère."

178

Sharing Secrets Between Generations

Some of us are "ancient-fashioned;" we still want to hear stories around the campfire, just as folks have done since cave people discovered flint could make sparks.

After five months of planning, Lifecircle finally happened last month in Menomonee Park. A group of about forty women and girls, age twelve to seventy-one, gathered for a storytelling camp-out.

Two friends and I organized the event, a first for our church, Good Shepherd in Menomonee Falls. Many of our ideas evolved during bike rides to Menomonee Park, where we eventually held the camp-out.

We didn't know what to expect of the weekend, and we were in for many surprises. Some of our pleasant discoveries:

Girls age twelve to seventeen really want to hear stories told by mothers and grandmothers. We weren't sure if tales of their elders would hold teens' attention. Yet according to their evaluations, they would have liked to hear more.

Girls have wisdom and insight into their own lives. They showed this during our camp icebreaker when they told how the stones that they had found on a hike were like themselves. While some of the women's comparisons were frivolous, almost all the girls' reflections were deep.

Girls aren't necessarily afraid to speak out in a large group that includes adults. Some of the younger ones did delay speaking until the end, but they shared willingly.

Girls enjoy music other than what they hear on MTV. They enjoy religious music, if it's fun or lively or beautiful. They liked what became our camp-out theme song, by Libby Roderick, that included these words:

"How could anyone ever tell you
you were anything less than beautiful?
... How deeply you're connected to my soul."

Many of our young campers had been part of an interdenominational Christian work camp earlier this summer, where they did home improvements for poor and elderly people. The girls' bell-clear voices rocked our campfire when they shared work camp songs they learned from other young volunteers.

And what of the stories told? We had all varieties, from lighthearted to serious. Yet you could take a lesson from every one, if you read between the lines.

Lessons included "Better to be engaged one hundred times than to marry the wrong man once" and "Look inside the person. Looks aren't important." There were many more lessons from stories that could have remained a secret. I keep thinking about the stories I heard. I can't wait until our next Lifecircle get-together.

Parents and grandparents, share your stories. Don't let them stay secrets.

[1997]

Going "Up North" is a kind of sacrament in Wisconsin. Goodbye, home duties. You'll wait for us.

In Praise of Silliness

If you are Romanian, New Year's Eve is the night for death threats. I learned this from my husband's Romanian relatives.

If you have a fruit tree that hasn't borne good fruit in years, you confront the tree at the stroke of midnight on New Year's Eve. You tie a rag around its trunk and knock the tree with a hatchet. You yell at the tree in Romanian, saying, "Either you bear fruit this year or I'll chop you down with this hatchet!"

Mike and I have used this threat. I think it produced more laughter than pears.

When I was a student in Rome, I learned a different New Year's Eve custom. The Italians gather the chipped china and ugly crockery they're sick of. They smash it on the ground and shout, "Happy New Year!" This tradition is richly symbolic: of the old ways you're giving up – and of the splinters you'll gather when you clean up the shards of dishes you broke.

We spent several Italian-style New Year's Eves with my parents, ages ago. I can still see my dad climb onto the kitchen counter and rummage around until he discovered old stuff deep in the back of the cupboards (Mum never threw anything out). He'd produce an ancient candy dish or ashtray, then with glee say, "I always hated this!"

I can picture Mum running after him, trying in vain to intercept him as he clutched his prize and headed for the concrete patio smashing ground.

I can still see Pop flinging the crockery to the ground, then double over chortling after butchering the Italian. (He had the right accent but never got the words right.) He laughed until tears streamed from his eyes.

181

Another silly tradition is the Polar Bear plunge: you jump into the coldest lake you can find. Some folks do this at midnight on New Year's Eve. I and other more, um, sensible Polar Bears jump in Lake Michigan off Bradford Beach in Milwaukee at noon on January 1. It's the only time the lake water feels warmer than the air. Walking after the plunge is interesting: your feet feel like concrete blocks.

No matter if they seem like nonsense, traditions are important. Ritual events speak to our hearts.

On New Year's Eve, I recommend going for the silly. Forget the resolutions. When you start the year doing something sufficiently ridiculous, the rest of the year should fall into place.

[1998]

I read that in many depressed people's brains, the quadrant governing PLAY has atrophied. Could PLAY be medicine for depression?

The Saga of the Notched Mousetrap

You never know what you're going to find when you come back home after a week's summer vacation. I'm always relieved to find the house still standing and no water in the basement. I never expected what I found this August.

I didn't notice it when we first returned. I was too busy unpacking, doing laundry, sorting mail, returning phone calls, and mowing the shaggy lawn. Then Monday through Wednesday, I was busy back at work, excavating the pile that had accumulated on my desk.

Thursday was my first day of slow-down, and the first day I noticed it: the smell of death. I got a whiff every time I passed through our front hall. But like cobwebs at a Thanksgiving dinner, the stench didn't manifest itself grandly until company arrived. Lucky for me, company was my very understanding neighbor, Chris Lodl.

"Do you smell something dead?" I asked her.

"I think I smelled something outside," she said. At the time, I wondered if this was a neighborly "save" on Chris's part, like the urban legend about the hostess who "accidentally" spills her wine after a guest spills wine on an expensive chair.

I was taking care of Chris's kids that day, so I gave young Nathan and Katrina the assignment of searching around the bushes outside for anything decomposing. We live in the country where wildlife abounds.

The kids found nothing.

But the odor persisted. And still I didn't guess its source.

The next day, Nathan and Katrina came over again, as did my grandbaby, Oliver. By now, the stench had become our constant companion. We searched again around the perimeter of the house, with no luck.

Finally the light went on in my head, but not a happy light – more like a light where you finally see the monster and you're really sad you looked. I belatedly realized that the stink must be coming from our mousetrap cupboard, even though we usually catch mice only during fall and winter.

The mousetrap cupboard is a small storage area above the stove where we discovered mice "dirt" (my mother's euphemism for turds) when we first moved in. New to the area, we learned that cold-weather rural homes often get an influx of rodent refugees when the frost snaps. Rather than caulk up cupboard crevices around the stove vent leading to the attic, Mike designated this as our mouse-catching place.

We cleared the cupboard and strategically placed mousetraps inside. Over the quarter-century since, the mousetraps have varied from old-fashioned wood-and-wire ones to plastic ones (inefficient) and humane ones (too hard to use). Peanut butter has always been the last meal of choice for our prey.

I cried the first time we killed a mouse. They're so cute, with those little ears. But after I found "dirt" in my silverware drawer, I quit crying. I simply avert my eyes when Mike marches the trap and corpse out of the house.

When our four-year-old daughter, Anna, discovered that we were catching mice in the cupboard, she decided to decorate the area for the critters. She grabbed her crayons and drew them a picture – it still hangs inside the cupboard door, seventeen years later. It's a portrait of a mouse. Strangely, the edges of Anna's paper have tiny chew-bites; some mouse must have found the drawing delicious.

There aren't a lot of household jobs that Mike "owns," but with most of them, his near-complete lack of a sense of smell comes in handy (although somehow toilet-cleaning and cat litter box-cleaning remain on my list). His jobs include catching mice, grilling meat, cleaning fish we catch, taking garbage to the curb, changing light bulbs, and cleaning the aquarium. Mike takes pride in all his jobs.

And, at fifty-six years old, he's becoming eccentric. For instance, he dates all light bulbs to see how long they last. He fillets the smallest bluegill. He has a special grill tower contraption that gets charcoal hot *fast*. He hasn't found a way to add weirdness to garbage duty, but I'm sure that's coming.

And the mousetraps – ah, the mousetraps. When he figured out which mousetraps worked best, he started *notching* them. Like a Western gunslinger who notched the handle of his pistol for every kill, Mike carves a notch into the wooden base of the trap for every mouse that has its last supper there. Unlike most people who throw away the trap with the mouse, Mike re-uses the device after dropping the corpse into the bushes and cleaning the trap.

Anyway, when I deduced that the smell of death was probably emanating from the mousetrap cupboard, I gingerly opened the cupboard door. I'm too short to see inside, but I did spy the corner of a trap and one mouse leg jutting up in unmistakable *rigor mortis.*

I slammed shut the cupboard door and started doing the shudder dance around the kitchen – "*Ew! Ew!*" I whined. Nathan and Katrina laughed at my dance, but Oliver cried. When I realized I had scared him, I snatched him up into my arms and he calmed down right away. I felt guilty for scaring a one-year-old with my own gross-out.

That night, I told Mike the whole mouse smell horror story, and he quickly moved to dispatch his quarry. When he opened the mousetrap cupboard

185

door, even he, the non-smeller, could detect the whiff of mortality.

"*Ew*," he said, but omitted the shudder dance.

I looked away. I didn't want to see the carnage.

Mike kept "*Ew*"-ing as he carried the trap outside.

Still looking away, I asked, "Are there any maggots?"

"Yes," he answered. "And the mouse and fur are all in pieces."

The combination of neglect and hot summer days must have done their parts in nature's work of decomposition.

Ew.

"Throw that trap out!" I hollered.

"No way! This is my lucky trap. I have to notch it!" he answered through the screen door.

I shook my head. I knew there was no use arguing.

A bucket of detergent water later, the cupboard smelled good again and the mousetrap was almost down to neutral.

The next day, our neighbor Mark and his friend Kenny stopped by to visit Mike and me, on their way to a thresheree/antique tractor show. We sat and talked a while. I raised the subject of the dead mouse.

"Can you believe he won't throw out the old trap? He has to notch it!" I complained. I should have known better than to complain to two unshaven guys in ball caps who were on their way to a tractor show.

Kenny said, "Great idea! Now you should find a way to date the notches!"

He and Mark and Mike spent the next ten minutes considering various ways to mark month and year on each notch – or would it be best to simply separate notches by years?

I practiced dissociation.

Soon the mousetrap got properly notched (though not dated like the light bulbs) and returned to its place in the mousetrap cupboard. Within three days, we caught another mouse. To our shock, it was one of the plastic traps that caught it. I thought Mike would empty the trap and return it to the mousetrap cupboard, unmarked. There was no way he could notch the hard plastic.

How wrong I was.

Busy with something else, I became aware of a funny noise coming from the basement. A few minutes later, Mike emerged, goofy grin on his face.

He had notched the plastic trap. With a hacksaw.

The real surprise after our week-long vacation wasn't the mouse in the cupboard. The real surprise was learning something new about this man I've been married to for thirty-four years: never underestimate a hunter's ingenuity in the face of a challenge.

[2006]

Every husband and wife experience love-waves for each other, not always at the same time and intensity. The trick is to ride the waves and enjoy them while they last.

Hosting a Souper Party

Many soups at souper party 2012
With Pauline Beck, daughter Anna, daughter-in-law Katie, Arleen
Hollenhorst, daughter-in-law Rachl, AJ Star, and Chris Lodl

My next-door neighbor Judy Dees says "Making soup is a spiritual experience."

I agree. I just hosted my second annual soup exchange party. Wisconsin is so weird. Last year we had our soup exchange in March and we wound up spending a lot of time outside on the deck; the temperature was in the sixties or so. This year we met again in March – but there was hardly enough room for my friends to park their cars around the plowed-up piles of snow in our driveway. So it goes in our beloved state.

No whether the weather, I'm always ready for soup. I never get sick of it – probably because there are so many different kinds. If you're sick of brothy soup, you can make one thick enough to walk across, and vice versa. If you're sick of vegetable soup, you can make meat soup, and vice versa. If you're sick of creamy soup, you can make a brothy one, and vice versa - on and on.

A friend told me about a Christmas cookie exchange she goes to every year. The participants are *very* strict about the rules. If you bring three dozen, you leave with three dozen. If you bring six dozen, you leave with six dozen. No variation. My cooking friends are much more loosey-goosey in giving out their soup. As my neighbor Chris Lodl says, "It's just *soup.*"

Last year we had eight cooks who attended the gathering, with soups featured from nine cooks (one couldn't make the party but sent her soup along). This year we had only six cooks, so we had less variety in soups.

However, this year we had more variety in age: the youngest was twenty-eight and the oldest was seventy-eight. Last year the youngest was twenty-seven and the oldest was sixty-four. The age difference is part of the fun. I've noticed that young and old take turns shocking each other. There are a *lot* of laughs.

I went to my first soup party in 2010, where we snacked on cheese and crackers, drank wine, and chatted before doing the exchange. At the two parties I hosted, I chose to serve a simple supper first: vegetarian chili and cornbread. We also had tea, coffee, strawberry shortcake, and some wine.

Someone suggested doing a "best soup" tasting and judging, but we can't quite figure out the logistics, with all the talking, laughing, eating, and imbibing we have to do. I think my friends are a little too relaxed for a juried event.

Here's how we do the exchange:

Any homemade soup is allowed, even if it's "homemade" by the local restaurant or grocery known for good soups. We don't judge.

189

The cooks put their soups into various quart containers: Ziploc bags (we found they hold a full quart and don't burst during freezing), rigid plastic store-bought containers, re-used deli containers, whatever.

Each soup is labeled by name; cooks indicate if it's vegetarian or not.

Some cooks freeze their soups ahead of time. We refer to Internet sources for wisdom about which soups freeze well.

Everyone puts their soups in a pile on my big dining room table, often with photocopied recipes nearby.

This year, my friend Arleen brought a container of her soup and warmed it so people could try it first; she wasn't sure if folks would like the ginger she used in it (we did).

Each cook tells a little about her soup – where the recipe came from, what alterations to the recipe the cook might have made, how the soup went over in her family, and so on.

Everyone draws a number. The person who drew Number One chooses a soup-to-go first, and so on.

Strictly speaking, if you come with five soups, you leave with five. But our group tends to share easily. People who bring more soups encourage those who brought fewer soups to take them anyway.

Folks take their souper treasures home. That's it!

[2013]

Sitting at the tractor pull in Markesan, I gazed around and became sure that there was not one man there who had done any "manscaping."

Part Seven
Living With Grief

The road to the Military Bridge in Michigan's
Upper Peninsula (Photo by Sally Grenier Yakel)

For Everything There is a Season, For Every Soul There is a Reason

Every April it happens: the waking earth brings me a mixture of joy and pain. New life bursts all around, stirring a memory I sometimes try to bury deep within myself. As winter loses its hold, I think again about what death taught me in the fullness of summer six years ago.

It was a glorious August day and I felt glad to be alive. In the backyard, I basked in the warm sunshine with my little sons Charlie and Brian. Then the phone call came that tore my life apart.

"Gail," my brother David choked on the other end of the line. "Come – home – now!" He sounded like he was being strangled.

I felt confused. "What's wrong, David? Are you all right?"

Again the choking voice, "Just come home!"

"Okay, I'll be right there." I hung up the phone as my stomach churned in sickened fear. What could be wrong with David? It was such an odd request – to come home. David was eighteen and lived at home with my parents, but I hadn't lived with them for six years. *This* was my home, ten miles away.

I raced next door to ask my neighbor Maureen to watch my baby, Brian, for a while.

"What's the matter?" she asked.

"I don't know. My brother David called and asked me to come home right away. He wouldn't tell me the problem. I've never heard him sound that way – like he was crying and couldn't breathe."

"Is he home alone?" Maureen asked.

"Yes. He stayed home while my folks went on a fishing trip with our little brother George."

192

Maureen's face fell. She told me to leave the baby with her as long as I needed to.

I felt like there was no blood left in my head. I kissed Brian goodbye and ran to the car with Charlie. I strapped him into his car seat. Then, putting the key into the ignition, I reminded myself to take deep breaths. Usually, I'm mechanically calm in a crisis. But this was different. I didn't know what was wrong.

The ten miles to my parents' house were the longest I ever drove. I was tortured with outrageous, horrible imaginings. Drug overdose, burning house? As I tried to keep my speed under sixty, I pictured David's girlfriend, Laura, dying in a plane crash. We all loved Laura like a sister, and I knew she had flown to Hawaii to visit her brother. But no, I thought. The truth can't possibly be as bad as my fears. I tried to comfort myself with the thought that the unknown is always more frightening than the known.

I was wrong.

When I drove into Mum and Pop's familiar driveway, everything looked normal. The house hadn't burned down. There were no beer bottles strewn on the lawn. The trees weren't strung with toilet paper. August was quiet, glorious, and sunny here, too. Mum's flowers bloomed in cheerful profusion. I took Charlie and ran into the house. Finding no one in the kitchen, I flew down the steps to the family room. David and my sister, Sally, were at opposite ends of the room, as if something invisible and enormous were wedged between them. They were both red-eyed and teary-faced, looking at me with terrifying pain.

I blurted, "David, is Laura dead?"

Sally burst into loud sobs. David looked like he was in agony. He gazed straight into my eyes and said the words my heart has played over a thousand times: "No – Mum and Pop and George."

Three days later, we had the vigil for my parents and brother. Hundreds of people filed through the funeral home. I remembered Mum and Pop saying that young people always have big funerals. I spent hours comforting people, many I hardly knew. Again and again, two red eyes and a handkerchief approached me. Again and again, two heavy arms encircled me in a trembling hug. And always variations on the same words: "Why did it have to be them? It's such a tragedy. They were so young and full of life. I still can't believe it. Such a terrible accident. I don't know what to say. And Georgie so young. Why was he even born?"

I felt the people's love for my parents and brother, but as yet, not their anger. My father had taught me to accept death; he was fond of saying "When your number's up, it's up." That philosophy helped me early on, when I experienced the natural numbness of shock. Anger would set in later when I could *feel* things again. In a week, I would want to kick in the walls to release my rage, but during the vigil that Friday night, I was still under emotional anesthesia.

I looked at the three caskets, quiet and unmoving on the floor. Closed caskets, made of fine wood – smooth, warm, and gleaming. I felt a comfort from that perfect wood, nature's beautiful design, magnificent grain. It made a silent statement. When all the visitors left, I laid my face on each casket in turn. Wrapping my arms around each one and hugging it, feeling the warm wood against my face, I let the tears flow.

This coming August will mark six years since Mum and Pop and George died. Sometimes, I wonder if the pain and tears will ever end. I ache still as I type this, and I don't want to think about them because the memories bring more pain. But there is something more to this tragedy. There is an answer for those angry, hurting people who wondered why George was born. I don't know why George died at age thirteen, or why my mother died at forty-eight and my father at fifty-one. I don't assume to know the plan of life. But

George's brief life wasn't a waste. I'm sure that one of the reasons George was born was to save my mother's life – just by being there in her womb.

My mother was a strong healthy woman who believed in never going to the doctor. She simply refused to get sick. But when she recognized signs of pregnancy for the fifth time, she made the familiar trip to her doctor. If Mum hadn't been pregnant with George, she never would have gone for medical attention, for a pelvic exam, for a Pap test. She probably would not have discovered she had cancer until it was too late. And chances are high that she would have died long before seeing her children grow up, and before experiencing the joy of grandchildren.

But George *was* there, and Mum *did* go to the doctor who *did* find the cancer in her uterus. Perhaps it was a miracle that George could be carried and born safely. Perhaps it was a miracle that the doctor could remove the cancerous growth from Mum's body a short time after George's birth. She was thirty-five then, and the cancer never returned; perhaps another miracle.

George was an inventor, musician, trouble-maker, jokester. He brought lots of laughter into our lives and some measure of pain to my parents. Mum and Pop experienced a case of "parent burnout" and frequently ran out of patience for George's typical youthful stunts.

My brothers and sister and I liked to tell George the story of how he saved Mum's life. We told him how we might have lost her when we were very young if it hadn't been for him. George wouldn't say much when we'd tell him this, but his eyes would twinkle and he'd stand a little straighter. Thank God we never kept our gratitude from him.

The angry, questioning people know now. I'm sure the Creator had a plan in George's conception. We were given a beautiful brother to enjoy for thirteen years and were blessed with our mother's continued nurturing during the years we really needed her.

It's true that my sons will never know their funny uncle who loved to put rubber worms into the cartons of his mother's cottage cheese. And they'll never be able to soak up the wisdom of their grandparents, except from stories I tell them. They'll have to wait until another life, like I will, to see Mum and Pop and George. Sometimes, when I sit in the April sun with my children, I think about these things. I hope I can teach them to accept life's plan: for everything there is a season, and for every soul there is a reason.

[1984]

A photo found in Pop's wallet after he died: Mum with Sally and David, circa 1965

Life isn't fair. We have to get used to it and get on with it.

The Wall

When I was sixteen, I did something rotten. It happened while I was working my first job, as a page in the Brookfield Public Library. One day my boss assigned me the task of updating records. I had to get rid of all index cards listing the names of inactive library patrons.

At some point, I came upon the name of a Brookfield boy who I knew had died in Vietnam. I pulled his card and threw it into the waste basket. It was a cold thing to do, and I've never forgiven myself. I should have carried that card home with me. I should have tucked it into a drawer or mailed it to his parents, anything but what I did.

Recently, I got my chance to make amends. The Vietnam Veterans Moving Wall came to Catholic Memorial High School in Waukesha, and I went there. I got paper and a black crayon and I rubbed across the name of that sailor from Brookfield who died at age twenty-one: William R. Glueckstein. The rubbing is propped on my desk.

I was a volunteer worker the first day The Moving Wall was here. For four hours, I leaked tears. It was different from crying. And it was good.

My husband stopped by after work that day and found me as I walked back and forth greeting visitors, helping them find names, handing out materials for rubbings. When Mike and I saw each other, we broke into big, shaking sobs. We stood a foot apart from each other, frozen but shaking, unable to take a step forward to hold each other.

"I have to go," Mike said.

"Don't you want to stay for the opening ceremony? It's going to be beautiful."

"I'll die,' he said. He left.

I saw veterans exchanging stories that day, standing in front of the names of their fallen comrades. I saw a man wearing a yarmulke and a shawl bowing and murmuring prayers as if he were at The Wailing Wall. I saw many people cry. You don't often see Americans weeping in public. It was like a funeral, the biggest funeral I've ever attended: the names of 58,201 men and eight women are etched into that monument.

I will never get over the bitter feeling in my stomach and the burning in my eyes when I hear the words "Vietnam War." But I am grateful to the veterans and volunteers who made The Moving Wall a reality for those of us who haven't had a chance to see The Wall in Washington, D.C.

Thanks to them, I have a rubbing of a name – one I won't throw away.

[1998]

War casts long shadows.

Generational Sadness
St. Michael's, Wisconsin

We save Grandma Hoerig's grave visit
for the last day of vacation.

We follow an order –
before the cemetery
we visit the family farmstead
down the road.

My eyes are ready for the
green stucco farmhouse,
a big square,
and the giant barn,
weathered red boards,
fieldstone foundation.

But this time is
different.

The fieldstones are there, still
piled on top of one another,
mortar sealing them.

But all around, rubble.
No barn,
just boards, strewn.

My eyes start stinging

even though it was
not I who played in that haymow,
not I who milked the cows before school,

even though it was

not my world that blew apart
when Grandpa Arthur died
at age 41,

even though it was
not my dream that died
when my mother began doing a woman's work
inside the big green stucco house
at age eleven,

even though it was
not my dream that died
when Grandma could no longer
handle the plowing and the milking,

even though it was
not my dream that died
when she auctioned off the farm
and moved to the city
with my mother.

My eyes keep stinging
the whole time I pull weeds from
Grandma's grave.

I blink and I blink.

Finally I let it out,
standing in that graveyard
where my mother and her brother
mowed the grass in happier days.

I stand alone and
weep
loud and hard
for all the dreams that died.

[2006]

Miracle

A man named Lloyd
drove his truck head-on
into my parents' car.
Mother, father, brother killed in an instant.
Lloyd had bad brakes and no license,
but for some reason I forgave him.

At the same time
my anger seethed and grew
against someone who hurt me.

Sometimes I wore my anger like a badge,
sometimes it weighed me down –
always it burned like a ball in my gut
for 25 years.

Someone said, "The past is over,
you can't change it,
forgive and forget –
bury your anger."

But I didn't want to bury it,
knowing its grave would lie
deep inside me.
I wanted my anger *lifted.*
So I prayed. And prayed.
But for 25 years
the anger never left my shoulders.

Then this week I learned
a man named Charles
walked into a schoolhouse
and shot five little Amish girls dead.

The parents of the girls
told the killer's family that
Charles is forgiven
for killing their babies.

This morning
I woke up and realized
my anger is gone – *lifted*
and fallen from my shoulders like a cloak.

Miracle

[2006]

*I have come to believe that forgiveness is the secret to
health – of mind and body.*

My Brother George, Dead and Alive

George, about twelve years old

Sometimes you go looking for one thing and you find another. It took me thirty years to face the place. When I faced it, love and pain came pounding down on me like a hailstorm. And I'm glad of it.

It was August 23, 2008: thirty years and one day after my parents and brother George were killed in a car accident on a bridge in Michigan's Upper Peninsula. It was time to look for that bridge I'd never seen.

I'd tried to visit once before. In 1998, the twenty-year anniversary of the crash, my brother David and I planned a trip in search of the place. But at the last minute, we both chickened out. We were afraid of the bridge. Plus, I'm superstitious. In August 1998, I was a bit shy of the age Mum was when she died – forty-eight. And my daughter was the same age George was when he died – thirteen. Why tempt fate?

And so 1998 faded, and the next year and the next, until another decade passed with nary a whisper of making a pilgrimage to the place that changed our lives forever.

Then, this past August, my husband and I stayed at a friend's cottage in Northern Wisconsin and realized we were less than two hours' drive from the scene of the accident. Because we hadn't planned to go there, I had no time to gather my fear. So on the last day of our vacation, Mike and I glanced at a map, jumped in the car, and started driving toward Bruce Crossing in Upper Michigan.

The highway became a waving banner flung over hills that grew more rolling. Thousands of towering evergreens stood sentinel as we passed. Our car was usually the only one on the road. Wildflowers blossomed in purple and yellow profusion along the roadside. This is what they were looking at, I thought, on the last day of their lives. All was beauty. This wasn't a scary place at all. The miles unfolded as scenes of my life with Mum and Pop and George swept through my mind.

I saw Pop teaching me how to dance the jitterbug and how to fish before dawn, by feel, without a bobber.

I saw Mum taking me to the store to buy a new dress after my boyfriend dumped me for his old girlfriend.

I saw George wrapping an arm around his two-year-old nephew, our son Charlie, as they rode a carousel together. George teased Charlie, calling him "Chowlie." Charlie teased right back, calling his uncle "Gorg."

I saw Mum jumping and laughing when she came upon the rubber worm George had planted in her cottage cheese.

As we neared Bruce Crossing, Mike and I spotted signs for waterfalls. "Remember someone said they must have been going to see a waterfall that day?" I asked Mike.

"Yeah, I remember," he said.

I saw Mum frowning as she told me she'd discovered that George had started fires in the attic while she and Pop were gone out of town. Mike and I had been in charge of George, and we hadn't been aware of his shenanigans.

I saw myself reading three autopsy reports and learning more than I wanted to know about sudden death and broken bodies.

I was talking to Mike casually, but not feeling casual. Could he tell? My body felt foreign, as if all my cells were humming. I propped my bare feet up on the dashboard, wiggled them, wiggled them some more in an effort to feel normal. Sadness filled my skin like awful collagen that needed to burst out. Yet my eyes weren't burning. The sadness was going to erupt not through tears, but through an explosion of some kind. I could tell by the humming.

I didn't explode. The sun shone and the wind rushed in through the windows as we drove along and searched for the bridge. Since this trip was spontaneous, we hadn't checked the old newspaper clippings in a scrapbook back home that would have pinpointed the death spot. Every time we crossed a bridge, Mike and I grew quiet. In my mind, the same questions replayed:

Is this the bridge? Following a curving stretch of highway? Would this be where a driver of a double-trailer semi would realize he couldn't slow down in time to avoid hitting a tractor in front of him? Would this be the spot where he'd veer around the tractor before seeing my folks' car coming from the opposite direction?

Is this where he'd ram head-on into that car and then push it backward a hundred feet to the base of the bridge? Is there a building at the bottom of the bridge, a truck stop or something, where people would have gathered, then heard the crash, then rushed out and looked into the vehicle to see three obviously dead bodies, before the car burst into flames?

Mike and I re-hashed these facts as we trundled over each bridge. Every time, I saw the accident in slow motion, a bit of imagination I've tried not always successfully to avoid during the past three decades. Even now as I type out the events of the crash, I have a gut-fantasy that if I type it differently, it won't have happened. I'm amazed that even three decades later, I can still experience denial and bargaining, two of the grief stages made famous by psychiatrist Elisabeth Kubler-Ross.

Besides the accident details, Mike and I recalled the names of two towns: Bruce Crossing, near the bridge, and Ontonagon, the county seat, where the truck driver was later tried and sentenced to three months in jail. He'd been driving with an expired license and faulty brakes.

We drove past Bruce Crossing, up and down hills into wilder country. Lots of bridges, but no curving road. And no bridge seemed scary; I couldn't imagine any being a death scene. To realize they died in such innocent-looking country reminded me of one of Pop's favorite sayings: "When your number's up, it's up." Their numbers were up. It wasn't easy to accept at the time, but I'd been trained by Pop's fatalism. I hoped only that they didn't suffer. It was a mercy when we got the coroner's report stating that they all died instantly.

After traversing many bridges, Mike and I came to a rest stop where we parked and stretched. We walked to the end of an old roadway that was cut off bluntly like a deck, right before it would require a bridge to span the Ontonagon River. We gazed down at the moving water.

The river was telling no secrets. "Let's turn around, Mike," I said. I was tired of the humming in my body, the slo-mo death scene in my head. I was weary of the feeling that I was about to explode.

Mike turned the car around and we retraced the rolling highway through the sunny afternoon. When we returned to the bridge that seemed the most likely one, we stopped at the general store at its base. Suddenly my sad-explode feeling melted. I became a sleuth digging for clues to a mystery I was ready to solve. I'd never spoken to anyone who was *there, that day.*

In the store, I asked the young woman behind the counter, "Did you ever hear of a big crash on that bridge thirty years ago involving a semi and a car?" I gestured out the window.

She reached to a low shelf and grabbed a yellowed newspaper article, then pushed it across the counter toward me. My stomach clenched when I read the headline: "Three die."

But it wasn't *our* three, and it wasn't thirty years before. Instead, the clipping told about an accident that had occurred there twenty years earlier. A semi had been barreling over the bridge outside the general store. The driver couldn't brake for a slow-moving delivery truck, so pulled left to pass. At that moment, the delivery truck started turning left to get to the store. Now turning parallel to the delivery truck and heading for the store, the semi driver slammed his brakes. The brakes screeched, alarming people inside the store. They rushed to the doorway at the same time as the semi crashed into the building: sudden death for one customer and the husband and wife who owned the store. Their numbers were up.

Mike and I left the store and drove across the highway to a tavern, also at the bottom of the bridge. This could have been the place where bystanders rushed out to investigate my folks' car. The brightness of the day seemed long gone the moment I entered the beer-scented tavern. An attractive older woman tended bar.

Mike ducked into the gents' room and I scooched onto a barstool. I ordered a beer, like all sleuths. You can't lurch into your interrogations – you have to go easy. After a few sips I asked the bartender the same question I'd asked at the general store.

"That guy over there might know," she said, indicating the short end of the bar.

I looked where she pointed. There was a gaunt man about eighty years old, standing with a group of younger men. He talked and gestured and puffed at a cigarette, his face deeply lined.

Pop could look like that now, I thought. He was a little guy like that man, and he'd be eighty-one. It didn't hurt my stomach to look at the man and imagine Pop that old. It felt good. It's a sort of parlor game I play with myself, wondering if Mum might look like that old lady, Pop like that old man. Mum and Pop never got grey hair. People complain about getting old, but I think it's a privilege. It's cool.

While Mum and Pop never got a chance to grow old, poor George never got a chance to grow up. He did save Mum's life, though. With confirmation of her fifth pregnancy – George – came the diagnosis that Mum had uterine cancer. Had she not been pregnant, she never would have visited the doc. Mum's thirteen-year-post-cancer survival matched George's thirteen years of life.

George. I sat and drank my beer. I'd been in a George phase for the past couple of years. Losing three at once, I take turns missing one more than the other. Grief comes in waves.

The bartender returned from talking to the old man and said, "He only remembers the truck that drove into the general store."

Mike joined me, laughed at my beer, and ordered a Coke. We finished our drinks and walked outside, blinking into sun glare. I snapped a picture of the bridge, in case it was the right one after all.

Birds sang. The bridge didn't look scary.

Mike and I returned to Wisconsin the next day. I dug out the scrapbook. Old newspaper clippings told details that would have helped us in Michigan: "The Greniers, who were on a fishing trip, were going north on Highway 45, five miles south of Rockland, Mich., when the collision occurred."

All Mike and I could piece together is that the rest area where we stopped and stretched, with the old road cut off like a deck at the river, might be the site of the original bridge. Maybe some time during the past thirty years, Michigan re-routed the road and built a new bridge because there were too many accidents on the original. Maybe it was a death trap. A scary bridge.

The map mystery was solved, but I'd unearthed papers I hadn't looked at in three decades: my brother's music. I sat alone for hours poring over George's handwritten song lyrics. At thirteen, he was already a songwriter – words *and* music. Maybe his youthful writing was influenced by our brother Dan, who was a musician; maybe it was because my parents had named him George Paul (after two Beatles, my suggestion in 1965 when he was born); maybe his soul knew he didn't have much time to leave a mark. Whatever the reason, George was destined for music.

He played with three buddies in a band they named "Diamonds." They played in garages, in basements, at parties. Ten days before he died, George played guitar and sang at our sister's wedding.

With the lyrics were photographs of George the rock star: looking into the eye of the camera, mouth wide, obviously wailing ("All right!" he wrote on the picture); singing with closed eyes to a pretend microphone; rocking hard on his guitar, shirtless; playing piano ("keyboards too!" his label for that shot). There were George's drawings of the band's van, jet, and boat, all with the Diamonds trademark. There were contract agreements designed by George, for George and his band mates.

I found cassette tapes with songs recorded by George and his friend Mark Hamilton: George's original songs as well as some covers of the Beatles and Kiss. Their voices are pure, cracking, adolescent.

I listened to the songs, staring at the pictures of George the young and beautiful. As I listened to the music and read the lyrics, I felt stunned again as I had years before at the depth of his feeling and at his choices of some words that seem eerie, prescient – words involving death, burning, a vehicle:

"Cape Cod Fisherman"
By George Grenier

Have you ever been to Cape Cod?
If not, you sure are missing a lot.
All the lucky fishermen
catching all the cod,
they don't even realize the beauty in the salt, of the sea.
But all of those fishermen, some have died
and some are born
and they're raised, by all the fish, the crabs, to be their fishermen.
Cape Cod fishermen have gone to rest, at home.
Cape Cod fishermen have gone to rest their souls.

Dedicated to David Grenier [our Uncle David, a Cape Cod fisherman]

"Phoenix"
By George Grenier

I know –
what you're thinking about me
and I don't –
have a chance to explain
I'm free – as a phoenix
You see –

I'm like a phoenix
in my nest
After 500 years
I burn to death
burn to death

You spice –
my nest
When I rest –
It turns –
It turns
to death
I'm as free –
as a phoenix
to die.

"War"
By George Grenier

I'm sittin at home, all free and clean,
a guy drives up in a black limousine,
I was afraid at the sight of that car,
for on the door, it said War ....

I'd forgotten George's lyrics except for those in "War." When I first heard that song after George's death in 1978, the words transformed in my mind, to

"A guy drives up in a white semi. I was afraid at the sight of that truck, for on the door, it said Death." It's always a white semi in my imagination. I hate white semis.

That night, after my hours-long communion with my brother George, I had a nightmare. This was the plot: *For $15.00, anyone can exhume a body from the cemetery. I hear about this and want to exhume George's body because I never saw it after the accident.* [I never saw my parents' bodies either, but this is a dream about George.] *I run fast in the dark, to the cemetery. Along the road are people kneeling next to caskets they've exhumed. They're removing cotton-like packing material from the caskets, but I see no corpses. Finally I have George's casket next to me. I open it and find the rock star pictures of him, with his muscular body and thick, wavy auburn hair. Next I find plastic zip-lock bags containing his bones, each labeled by type. I get only as far as little tiny bones.*

I woke from the dream and began to hyperventilate. Not wanting to wake Mike, I crept out of bed and padded outside into the warm night that was black as the cemetery nightmare.

There were choking sounds, like a door creaking, like gargling. There were animal growls. There were tears. The noises were punctuated by hyperventilating. All coming from me, somewhere far away.

The explosion.

When the sounds stopped, I returned to bed. I donned bedclothes, which I never wear. I tugged covers over my head, which I never do. I curled into a fetal ball. It was a warm summer night, but I wasn't too hot. I fell into a deep, black sleep.

When George died, I was twenty-seven years old, the mother of a two-year-old and a newborn. Long before the accident, Mum and Pop asked Mike and me to be George's legal guardians if they died. We said yes. When George died with them, I was devastated, but I admitted to myself something that filled me with guilt: I felt I couldn't have handled him. I knew he had some rough years ahead; he was already experimenting with smoking cigarettes. I barely knew how to handle my two-year-old, and I was breastfeeding a two-month-old. What would I do with a teenager?

I had terrible guilt for feeling some relief that I didn't have to raise a somewhat wild, grieving thirteen-year-old. My guilt lasted for years until one night, walking alone outside, I "talked" to George and asked him to forgive me. I didn't feel his presence at the time, just the guilt and sadness. It seemed right to shout into the lonely night, "I'm sorry, George, that I didn't want to raise you when you were thirteen."

After I shouted my apology, I felt immediate forgiveness and relief. That feeling has lasted. Now I just miss him. He'd be forty-three if he were alive. Middle-aged. My dear friend Tina Tierney is forty-three, and there's no "generation gap" between us, although I'm fifty-seven. Sometimes I tell her, "You're my George."

But of course she isn't.

It's October now. Recently, Mike and I enjoyed a fish fry at a friend's church. There, our friend introduced us to Pete Beaudoin, a guy in his early forties. We learned that Pete attended the same grade school as George.

"Did you know George Grenier?" I asked him.

Pete's eyes widened. "We used to play in the same band."

I told him how I'd unearthed George's tapes and song lyrics. Pete said he has some flyers from the old band days. We exchanged phone numbers.

I loved talking to Pete. In him, I saw a person in the full power of his manhood, where George would be now if he had the chance to grow up. Like seeing the old man in the bar at Bruce Crossing, it made me feel good, not sad.

The trip to the bridge, the scrapbook, the songs, the nightmare, meeting Pete, all made me realize how much grief I hold inside me, grief as raw as it was in 1978. I realized too how many questions I have about the crash and the trial of the driver. My brothers and sister and I were so young that we accepted it when the lawyer said, "You don't want to know what was said at the trial; you don't want to see the pictures of the car."

I looked up Lloyd, the semi driver, on the Internet. He's still alive, still living in Michigan. He's eighty-two, one year older than Pop would be now. I wish him no ill will, never have. Maybe I'll write him and tell him that. Maybe he'll write back and say, "I'm sorry."

I'd like to go back to the Upper Peninsula and find out if that highway was re-routed, and why. I'd like to go to the courthouse and read the trial transcripts. Then I'd know what was said and by whom.

I want to put all of George's songs on a CD and print out the rock star photos of him and make a booklet of his hand-written lyrics, like Neil Young's. I want people to listen to his songs and read his words and marvel at his beautiful soul.

Most of all, I'd like to do something I cannot do: touch George, and my parents too. Elisabeth Kubler-Ross wrote that in the event a body is disfigured by death, it's important for loved ones to see part of it, even if only a hand, for instance. She's right. I would have known Mum's hand, Pop's hand, George's hand. But I never saw anything. For all I know, they're gone on a very long vacation and we buried empty boxes.

After they died, the postcards came:

From George: "M and P go fishing all the time and I go once in a while but usually I just drive the boat. It's pretty fun cause we are not in the tent."

From Mum: "Greetings from Michigan. Had a beautiful day driving up here. Now if the fish bite it'll be heaven."

I may never go back to find the real bridge, or write to the truck driver, or make an album of George's music. It doesn't matter. Until my own number is up, I've learned to live with mystery. All I did this summer is open clouds and let hailstones pound my head. It hurts, but it's okay. I feel close to George as I write this. He's dead and alive.

[2008]

Years after Mike and I searched for it, my sister Sally found the bridge: Military Bridge in Ontonagon County. (Photo by Sally Grenier Yakel)

I have come to believe that our deceased loved ones are our guardian angels, and that they listen to us.

The Good They Die Young

You wonder about sayings like "The good they die young." And then you meet someone like Liz Nickel. And then she dies.

Liz's memorial was held last night. It was quiet and unassuming, like Liz. She would have liked it.

I met Liz ten years ago, when my husband and I fell in love with Cajun music. Our friendship with Liz and her husband Tom became linked with all things Cajun.

My favorite memories of Liz center around an old stove in an old schoolhouse at Folklore Village in Dodgeville, Wisconsin: Liz and I and a few other diehard Cajun-cooking-learners are taking turns stirring a big cook pan of roux. Despite our energetic stirring, the roux is remaining obstinately pale. So we stir some more, and talk. And laugh. And stir. And laugh some more. Finally the roux is good and brown, "Cajun fudge." Then our teacher Jackie Miller, from Iota, Louisiana, shows us how to use that roux in a gumbo.

We eat. And talk and laugh some more.

After several years of meeting at Folklore Village Cajun weekends, plus dancing at Cajun gatherings in Oshkosh, Wisconsin, and at Amana Colonies in Iowa, some of us from the Greater Milwaukee area began meeting to make Cajun music. We got together about once a month and spent hours playing almost-good Cajun tunes. I wanted to learn the triangle (the traditional Cajun percussion instrument), and I did, but I was pressed into service singing because I was the only one who knew any French. Joke was on me. My French knowledge turned out to be a deficit because Cajun French is very different from the French we learned back in high school. I had to un-learn one to learn the other.

216

Tom Nickel was already an accomplished musician ("Big Nick and the Cydecos") on guitar and accordion, and he began teaching himself fiddle. Leslie Jahnke played guitar, and she started working on accordion. My husband Mike learned to tingle away on the triangle without breaking anyone's eardrums. Players came and went, the group stayed small, and ever so slowly, the music sounded better.

Liz was quiet at first. Very quiet. But eventually she started singing along. Softly, then with more vigor. She never got to the point of belting – and you have to belt in order to be heard above the accordion – but she sang.

I remember singing with her and looking into her eyes as we went along. For a few verses of a tune, all I could feel was Liz and me, and we were doing it by golly even though we weren't doing it perfectly and we knew we'd never perform. There was a magic there. I'm sure she felt as happy as I did.

Once, at Folklore Village, I told Liz that I had spotted a church rummage sale sign. Next thing you know, Mike and I bumped into Liz at the rummage during a break from Cajun dancing and cooking lessons. We shopped side by side and laughed at ourselves. In Liz's obituary are the words "She was an avid thrift store shopper and collector of ensuing treasure." Ensuing treasure: I like that. I'll have to remember that next time I pick up something I hadn't realized I needed.

Over the years at Cajun gatherings, Liz and I had a lot of talks. We bemoaned our fates constantly fighting the battle of the bulge. She talked about how important music was for her husband, Tom. She wanted him to keep making music because it's the thing that makes the world right for him.

From time to time, Liz complained about being not-this or not-that. She wasn't a good enough dancer or whatever. She was probably the most self-effacing person I've ever met. I assured her that she was fine the way she was, but I think she kept her doubts. However, she never let those doubts interfere with her big smile and her big warmth. She always greeted me – and everybody else – with her smile and her warmth like a big blanket. I always felt so glad to set eyes on her.

At her memorial last night, I learned about a Liz I never knew. Liz's sister told about a young girl who was confident in her strength, a tomboy who was always "at the top of the tree." Liz loved nature and never met an animal she didn't find interesting.

It hurt my heart when I learned about Liz's natural athleticism, because that is the thing that was taken from her. A few years back, Liz told me that she was experiencing odd episodes of weakness. "It seems like MS or something," she said. She gradually found it harder to walk and harder to dance. I've had my foot in a surgical boot for a week now and can hardly stand my handicap. I can't imagine how difficult it must have been for Liz to keep up her spirits when she had to use a walker, when she fell and had to get stitches in her face, or when she couldn't get out of bed.

It wasn't MS. After many tests, doctors determined that Liz had Parkinson's disease. My neighbor is in his eighties and has had Parkinson's for ten years. I anticipated a similar long struggle for Liz.

But her slide was precipitous. I saw her in living snapshots a year apart, because we saw her only at Folklore Village. She became a watcher rather than a dancer. I never saw Liz between big Cajun events because I had left the Cajun jam band. I had realized that I didn't have enough time in the week to dedicate myself both to being a writer and also to doing the hard work of learning Cajun French well enough to sing.

I should have made the effort to go and visit, but I never did. You know how you have friends in their own little niches? Well, Liz was my Cajun-event-friend. She lived about forty-five minutes or so away from me, and I'm sorry I didn't try harder to see her between Cajun gatherings. Who would have known the disease would take her so soon? Every year Mike and I got a Christmas card from Tom and Liz. There was always a beautiful personal note. I long ago gave up sending Christmas cards. I didn't send a card. I didn't call. I'm sorry, Liz. I'm sorry, Tom. I am a fair-weather friend, but I did love Liz, and I am so sorry to have her gone from this earth.

Recently Tom joined the Cajun Strangers band and wrote a beautiful sad Cajun waltz (there is no other kind) for Liz. It's called "Elizabeth." As she requested, he played it at her memorial. He provided a recorded version because, he said, "This is a tough room to play."

The waltz threaded through the air of the room, all sad fiddle. Images of Liz flashed on a screen as the waltz wafted. There was the young strong Liz, all muscle, with a stringer of fish. There she was wearing a long braid while she stood in the foreground of a mountainous terrain. There she was, older, at Folklore Village with some of the rest of those who love this strange Cajun music that doesn't flow in our blood but flows in our souls.

And there were Tom's words flashing across the screen:

When God created us
He made people of every sort
but He never told me
that as I tread my journey
through life...
The very best people
that He created are not
nobility or "Movie Stars."
They are the quiet

and frequently invisible ones
who work hard and give
to others
rather than to take
for themselves
and Elizabeth
was one of them.

I heard Tom talking to Brian, one of his Cajun Strangers band mates. Tom was trying to put into words how it felt to lose his best friend and love who he'd had for what he called "the best twenty-three years" of his life. He said that it was like he and Liz had shared one brain. Now that she's gone, it's like part of his body is gone. He kept trying to describe the feeling, but he couldn't.

When words fail, music enters. Music will help Tom heal, and Liz will be smiling. She wanted him to make music.

This March, when we stir the roux at Folklore Village Cajun weekend, we will talk about Liz. We will laugh and we will cry.

Everyone at the memorial service talked about how Liz put the needs of others ahead of her own. She did anything to help anyone. That didn't surprise me. She chose to leave her brain to medical science for the research of Parkinson's disease in the hopes that a cure may be found for others. That also didn't surprise me.

Liz's family is huge (nine kids in her family of origin). A very small girl sat in front of us. We learned that she bears an honor. Her parents named her Elizabeth.

Dance lightly with body so light, Liz.

[2013]

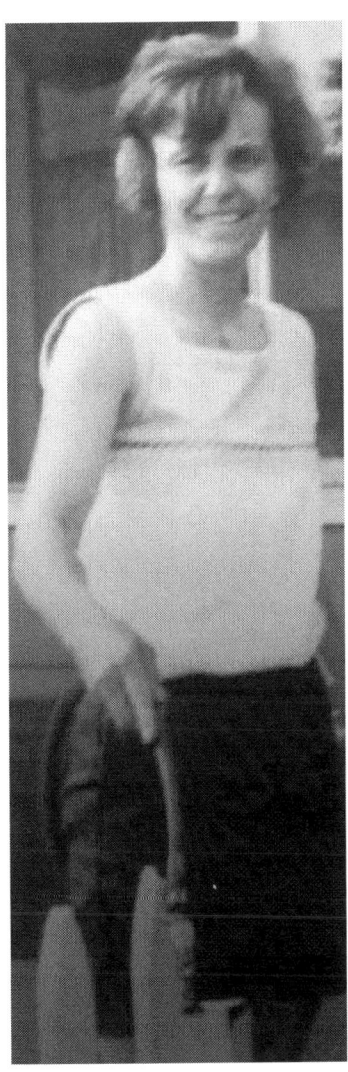

Remembering a Mother
Who Died too Young

This is how I spend time with
my mother –

I dance the tango
and remember her bossa nova
I harmonize
because she always did
I paint walls in my house
and see her wearing sandals
all splattered
I water my plants
and picture her hospital
for violets
I tie on an apron
and laugh –
she was too modern for
aprons
I cook
and taste her every-Monday
spaghetti
I watch the white grow into
my hair
and see her tiny fountain of
grey
I play with words
and hear her wordplay
I speak mangled German
every word from her
I love my husband and my children
and feel the love she gave us

I hug my grandchildren
for her

[2013]

221

A Postscript for Maureen and Me

My friend Maureen Fitzsimmons-Vanden Heuvel and I
made a pact: whoever dies first will be treated to an
Irish jig danced on her grave, performed by the one
who survives.

With Maureen Fitzsimmons-VandenHeuvel, 2013

Discussion Questions

1. For the author, dessert comes in many forms – nature, dancing, children, and so on. What do you think of her ideas of dessert?

2. What is your own idea of dessert?

3. The author says love is spelled T-I-M-E. How can you make time for what you consider the important things in your life – your "desserts?"

With "adopted" granddaughter Alaina, Milwaukee Domes, 2013
(Photo by Colleen Thomas-Lovelace)

About the Author

With husband Michael Sweet, September 2013
(Photo by Alexis Zimmerman)

Since 1977, Gail Grenier has written for the public. Her prize-winning column was syndicated, and her blog *Gail Grenier Here* gets thousands of hits. Gail lives with her husband, Michael Sweet, on ten acres in Menomonee Falls, Wisconsin.

GailGrenierSweet.com
Blog: Gail Grenier Here

Made in the USA
Middletown, DE
23 October 2021

50676488R00142